PICTORIAL HISTORY
OF THE LUFTWAFFE

BY THE SAME AUTHOR:

Instruments of Darkness
German Air Force Bombers
of World War Two (*two vols.*)

PICTORIAL HISTORY
OF THE
LUFTWAFFE
1933-1945

FLIGHT LIEUTENANT

ALFRED PRICE

ARCO PUBLISHING COMPANY, INC.

NEW YORK

Published by ARCO PUBLISHING COMPANY, Inc.
219 Park Avenue South, New York, N.Y. 10003

Library of Congress Catalog Number 73–96766
Standard Book Number 668–02144–6

Printed in Great Britain

Contents

Foreword

by LEN DEIGHTON

It is a curious fact that a quarter century after the Second World War, and in spite of a profusion of documents, recordings, photographs and films, the facts remain so elusive. So many books repeat the same propaganda fantasies that were manufactured by both sides for a wartime public starved of news.

The *Luftwaffe* bombing of Rotterdam in May 1940, in which high explosive bombs were dropped within a carefully defined target area upon Dutch army units, is a good example of an event which is consistently misreported. The bombers were already over the Dutch/German frontier when the Germans received an answer to their request for capitulation. The Dutch commander, Colonel Scharroo, had been deliberately evasive in his answer and was still requesting the name, rank and signature of the German commander. Acting immediately upon receipt of Scharroo's equivocal answer the Germans were able to divert 43% of the attacking aircraft to other targets. Nine hundred people died. That's nine hundred too many, but it's not the brutal and treacherous massacre of thousands of Dutchmen that Churchill's *The Second World War* describes or the mass bombing of the city that another historian writes Hitler ordered as an act of pure brutality and spite. Oddly the bombing of Belgrade, which was much more open to description of *Schrecklichkeit*, is seldom described. Mr. Price corrects the omission.

The statistics of war have always provided wonderful material for propaganda distortions and the air war's statistics were particularly tempting. Still today there are writers scorning the idea that 35 *Luftwaffe* pilots could have scored 150 or more victories during World War Two, perhaps because the top Anglo-American ace was credited with only 41. A close inspection of the records, however, serves only to support the *Luftwaffe* claims. The confirmation procedure was meticulous and Teutonic and its accuracy was confirmed by postwar research. It seems that many writers prefer to give their readers ancient but palatable propaganda instead of research and reality.

How excellent then, that this Pictorial History of the *Luftwaffe* should be in the expert hands of Alfred Price. Price, a serving aircrew officer, is an expert on all aspects of the *Luftwaffe*. I had known his work from technical journals for some time before I began my own small research into German nightfighter techniques, but I found that all enquiries led me back to this same man. Jack Beaumont in his famous aeronautical bookshop produced for me *Instruments of Darkness* with the solemn words, "This chap Price knows all the answers". The Imperial War Museum told me of him and so did the RAF Historical Branch. Later in Germany ex-*Luftwaffe* pilots and technicians told me that there were many questions about the *Luftwaffe* that Herr Price could answer more fully than they could. I was honoured and delighted therefore when he asked me to write this Foreword for his most impressing book.

It's no small feat to relate the history of the *Luftwaffe* in such a compact form and yet here are the personalities, equipment, aircraft and even the military background to the *Luftwaffe's* changing fortunes in the decade of its official existence. This well produced volume is distinguished not only by an authoritative text but also by over 200 carefully chosen photographs, many of them new to me. And here let me give thanks to the author for his really excellent and painstaking captions. Those of us who are waiting for Price's massive multi-tome *Luftwaffe* History will gladly use this until that definitive work is complete.

Introduction

WHATEVER one's political persuasion, there is much one can find that is intriguing about Hitler's *Luftwaffe*. Here was a force that in six short years rose almost from nothing to become the terror of Europe. It was the *Luftwaffe* that made possible the early lightning victories by the German Army. Then, gradually but inexorably, the air forces of Germany's enemies became stronger than her own, and the *Luftwaffe* was forced on to the defensive on each front in turn. Finally, the vast majority of its aircraft grounded for want of fuel, many of its best crews dead or in prison camps, the greater part of it could do no more than sit on the ground and wait for the end to come. But as long as the war lasted the *Luftwaffe* could never be ignored in the Allied calculations, for to the very end it proved capable of springing uncomfortable surprises.

For much of the time the primary task of the *Luftwaffe* was to provide aerial support for the German Army; for this reason it has been necessary to include brief descriptions of some of the ground battles in the text, so that the reader will be able to appreciate the background to the air operations.

I should like to thank William Kimber Ltd for allowing me to quote from Albert Kesselring's autobiography, Messrs Methuen and Co. for permission to use the passage from the book *The First And The Last* by Adolf Galland, and Robert Hale Ltd for permission to quote from *Broken Swastika* by Werner Baumbach.

The task of amassing the necessary photographs for this work would have been difficult indeed had it not been for the generous assistance of so many of my good friends. In particular I should like to express my gratitude to Hanfried Schliephake, Hans Obert, Franz Selinger, John Taylor, Eddie Creek, Philip Moyes, Martin Windrow and Gerhard Joos. Also I am indebted to the very helpful people administering the photographic collections at the Imperial War Museum and the Radio Times Hulton Picture Library.

A book of a serious nature is almost impossible without a measure of domestic tranquillity when the work is in progress, and I should like to take this chance to thank my wife, Jane, for bringing the endless cups of tea and fending off the children long enough for me to write this.

ALFRED PRICE

Tickhill, November 1968

CHAPTER ONE

Preparation

The lines of my policy have not been to create an offensive air arm which might constitute a threat to other nations, but to provide Germany with a military air force strong enough to defend her at any time against aerial attack.

Hermann Goering on March 8th, 1935, following the announcement that the Luftwaffe *was already in existence.*

UNDER the Treaty of Versailles, which ended the First World War, Germany was obliged to disband her air force and cease the manufacture of military aircraft. However, the treaty was not as effective as it might have been, for after a few months there were only a few limitations on the manufacture of civil aircraft, and by 1926 even these had been lifted. As in other countries at this time, several small airlines sprang into being, as did a number of flying schools to meet the demand for pilots.

To meet the demand for aircraft a small but efficient aircraft industry emerged, and by the mid-1920's the firms which were later to mass produce aircraft for the *Luftwaffe* all existed: Junkers at Dessau, Heinkel at Warnemünde, Dornier at Friedrichshafen, Focke-Wulf at Bremen. And at Augsburg the young Willy Messerschmitt was designing sporting aircraft for the Bavarian Aircraft Company.

While these developments were taking place, several ex-Imperial Flying Corps officers now serving in the German Army continued to interest themselves in aviation. In this they enjoyed the support of the Chief of the General Staff, General Hans von Seeckt, who saw to it that the closest links existed between his service and the Civil Aviation Department of the Ministry of Transport.

The Paris Air Agreement of 1926 placed severe restrictions on the number of German service personnel who were allowed to fly, but von Seeckt found little difficulty in evading these, and managed to build up a secret reserve of trained flying men. Through his service's contacts with the Civil Aviation Department, he was able to arrange for service pilots to be trained in the schools established by the German airlines. However, in Germany itself realistic military flying training was almost impossible without arousing suspicion, and to overcome this problem the Germans concluded a secret agreement with the Russians which allowed them to set up a training school at Lipetz, south of Moscow. Later a second school was set up in the Caucasus area. From 1926 on these turned out small numbers of trained fighter and reconnaissance pilots. At this time the Germans were preoccupied with defensive measures against a possible air attack, though they gave a lot of thought to operations in support of the ground forces. From German records we know that almost all the officers who later reached the senior ranks of the *Luftwaffe* did, at some time, pass through these Russian schools.

Thus some of the ground work for the creation of an air force had already been completed when Hitler came to power in Germany in March 1933. Hitler's deputy in the Nazi party was the forty-year-old ex-World War One fighter ace Hermann Wilhelm Goering, who one month later became the nation's Air Minister. Suddenly the building of the German air force received a new impetus. But this was far from being his only task in the new government, and Goering had to leave much of the work to his second in command, another ex-Imperial Flying Corps man, General Erhard Milch.

The task facing Milch in 1933 was immense, but he proved equal to it. His plan was to set up six bomber, six fighter and six reconnaissance *Geschwader*,* to be employed primarily as the nuclei for the training of still larger numbers of flying and ground crewmen. By this time the German aircraft industry had already begun experimenting with its first military aircraft since the war, and it was from these that Milch selected the equipment for his force. Milch regarded the first combat aircraft as interim types: they would serve his purpose merely by opening up the production lines, and providing his crews with experience with reasonably modern aircraft.

The first fighter type for the new air force was the Heinkel 51, a biplane with a maximum speed of 210 m.p.h.† and an armament of two rifle-calibre machine-guns. Milch ordered two bomber types, the Dornier 23 and the Junkers 52. Each of them had been developed from an aircraft originally designed as an airliner; that such a conversion could be made easily demonstrates the ineffectiveness of a treaty at that time designed to allow civil but not military flying. Nor were the two German bomber types in any way second-rate machines. Both were cantilever monoplanes incorporating what were then modern ideas in streamlining; they were both some tens of miles per hour faster than the equivalent Handley Page Heyford which made up the backbone of the Royal Air Force's bomber arm, and compared favourably with it in range and load-carrying ability.

But, as might be expected in a rapidly expanding air force, at first the main emphasis was on training machines. Under the initial plan almost half the

* For details of the unit organisation of the *Luftwaffe,* see Appendix A.
† In this it was some 25 m.p.h. slower than the Gloster Gauntlet then entering service with the Royal Air Force.

numerical strength of the *Luftwaffe* was made up of trainers, for the most part Focke-Wulf 44's, Arado 66's and 69's.

Having ordered his aircraft, Milch set about getting men of the calibre he needed. It was not easy. Neither the army nor the navy was keen to part with its best brains but Goering, through Hitler, was able to overcome such opposition. Whether the men themselves wished to transfer to the new arm was of little moment. The then Oberst * Albert Kesselring later wrote:

'When, in September 1933, Oberst Stumpff sought me out during a day-and-night exercise at manoeuvres with the object of interesting me in the appointment of Administrative Director of the future *Luftwaffe* he got a very lukewarm response. I wanted to stay with the army and recommended that the administrative work of the aeronautical section, and later of the *Luftwaffe*, should be taken over by the army. The matter was settled that evening at a mess dinner, however, at which the foreign military attachés and the Chief of the General Staff of the army were our guests. When I presented myself to Generalleutnant Baron von Hammerstein the following conversation ensued:

"Has Stumpff told you about your future employment?"
"Yes."
"Well, are you satisfied about it?"

When I said no and proceeded to summarise my reasons he cut me short with:

"You are a soldier and have to obey orders." ' †

In March 1935, exactly two years after he had gained power, Hitler felt secure enough to reveal his previously secret air force to the world. At this time the force comprised 1,888 aircraft of all types, and mustered 20,000 officers and men. Units which had been concealed as 'flying clubs' or 'police formations' now came out into the open and were handed over to the *Luftwaffe* one at a time in a series of ceremonial parades, many of which were attended by Hitler himself.

The new air force's programme of training and expansion now accelerated, and within a short time it had set up its own staff college, a very efficient signals service, and also its own *Flak* arm ‡ which became responsible for defending the German cities against air attack. From the very start the Germans laid great stress on the rapid mobility of their flying units and ground supporting units, and their operation at short notice from temporary landing grounds. The techniques developed were to serve the *Luftwaffe* well during the early

* For a comparison of German, British and American air force ranks, see Appendix C.
† From *The Memoirs of Field Marshal Kesselring*, published by William Kimber, London. Kesselring soon overcame his disappointment, and later rose to the rank of Chief of Staff of the new air force.
‡ *Flak*, short for *Fliegerabwehrkanonen*, meaning 'anti-aircraft guns'.

years of the war, when they enabled theatre commanders to bring decisive concentrations to bear in selected areas.

The 1930's saw a major revolution in the design of aircraft. From the fabric-covered biplane with its fixed undercarriage the major air forces shifted, some faster than others, to the fast monoplane with fully cantilevered wings, a retractable undercarriage, variable pitch propellers and all-metal stressed skin construction. Apart from the purely constructional features, there were other developments which were to have a profound effect upon air warfare. The development of instrument flying was one of these, for it made it possible for pilots to operate under conditions of marginal visibility, and thus greatly extended the operational flexibility of the aircraft. No less important were the advances in electronics which made possible a whole family of radio navigation aids and, in 1936, radar.

These developments combined to bring about an upheaval in all the major air forces. How did they effect the *Luftwaffe* in particular?

By 1936 the aircraft comprising the second generation of German combat aircraft had begun flight testing, and by the end of 1938 most of them were in service in quantity. The standard interceptor was the Messerschmitt Bf 109,* and the twin engined Messerschmitt Bf 110 was introduced as a long range bomber destroyer. The standard heavy bombers were the Dornier 17 and the Heinkel 111, to be supplemented later by the Junkers 88. The standard short range dive bomber was the Junkers 87. All these types included all the most modern design features, with the exception of the rugged Ju 87 which retained the fixed undercarriage.

To develop and teach the latest blind and long range flying techniques, Oberst Edgar Petersen set up a special flying school at Wesendorf near Hanover. Once a week, by day or by night, a Ju 52 heavily laden with fuel would take off to make the ten-hour 1,300 mile non-stop flight direct to Castel Benito, in what was then Italian Libya, or back. Each aircraft carried one instructor and three students, and during the flight the latter had to navigate using dead reckoning, astro navigation and, when these could be picked up, radio beacons. Such flights, which were near to the limits of what was possible in 1936 and 1937, provided extremely valuable training in long range navigational techniques.

In the field of electronics, also, the Germans were well advanced. During the early 1930's the Lorenz Company had developed a blind approach system to help aircraft to find their landing grounds in darkness or poor visibility; the system employed two adjacent radio beams to mark out a path extending a distance of up to thirty miles from the airfield. In the left hand beam Morse dots were transmitted, and in the right hand one dashes. The signals inter-locked, so that where the beams overlapped a steady note was transmitted: aircraft then navigated by flying down the steady-note zone until they came to

* Bf stood for *Bayerische Flugzeugwerke*—Bavarian Aircraft Company—where Willy Messerschmitt's designs were produced.

the beams' transmitter. By the mid-1930's the 'Lorenz' system was widely used, not only in civil airlines but in some air forces as well. The Royal Air Force ordered it, as did the *Luftwaffe*. But the Germans developed the Lorenz beam system further, and by 1939 two long range radio navigation and bombing aids had resulted: the *Knickebein* and the more precise *X-Geraet*. Both systems were unique to the *Luftwaffe*, and represented a commanding lead in technology until the British GEE system appeared in 1941.

In radar, too, the Germans made great strides. The German Navy began work with pulsed radar in 1936, within a few months of the first trials in Britain. By 1938 the *Freya* early-warning radar had entered service, a set superior in some respects, inferior in others, to the British 'Chain Home' radar of similar vintage. And by 1939 a second German radar, the *Wuerzburg* gun-laying set, entered service; its performance was better than any comparable set in Britain. But on the other hand the British had the lead in radar sets small enough to be installed in aircraft: they had two types, one for coastal patrol aircraft and one for night fighters, both on the point of entering service. It was not in radar hardware that the British had established their lead, but rather in the way in which the information was used: only in R.A.F. Fighter Command was a system developed before the war for channelling reliable and up-to-date information based on radar plots to fighter pilots by radio. The Germans made no attempt to perfect such a system prior to the war. Since they had then little to fear from hostile bombers, they logically concentrated their energies on more offensive developments—like the advanced radio beam navigational systems.

But if the Germans were well up with the most modern aeronautical and scientific developments, there were some glaring shortfalls in the more mundane field of supply. For example, as late as the summer of 1937 the *Luftwaffe* did not possess a single up-to-date bomb; production had still to begin. When this was revealed to Hitler during a briefing on the status of the armament programme there was a stony silence. A few days later the *Fuehrer* sent for Goering and some of the senior air staff officers. Hitler's intuition solved problems brilliantly on some occasions, but this was not one of them. He had, he said, given a lot of thought to the shortage of bombs: 'Germany has more than enough of those metal cylinders used for oxygen, acetylene, etc. We can fill them with explosives and use them as bombs!' One of the *Luftwaffe* officers pointed out, with respect, that the idea would not work: the cylinders had an appallingly bad ballistic shape, and could not be aimed properly—if they were released from an aircraft they would tumble erratically through the air. But Goering was quick to seize this opportunity to make good the face he had lost during the previous conference: 'My *Fuehrer*, may I express my thanks for this wonderful solution! I must admit that none of us could have thought of such an ingenious idea! You, and you alone, have saved the situation. Good Lord, to think that we're all such dumb-bells! I shall never be able to forgive myself!' In the face of this enthusiastic acceptance of the impossible by their leader, there was nothing the dumbfounded staff officers could say. When Germany went to war in 1939 there was still a desperate shortage of bombs, though in the event the problem had been largely solved by the time protracted and large scale air operations began the following year.

In itself the incident of the bombs was trivial, and had no real effect upon the course of the war. But it brings two important points into sharp focus. First, one sees Goering trying desperately to tell Hitler what he thought Hitler wanted to hear, rather than what he knew to be true; the habit was to prove almost impossibly difficult to break later. Second, it is clear that not until the very last moment did Goering—or most of the senior *Luftwaffe* officers for that matter—believe that there was really going to be a large scale war; and if there was no war, what difference did it make if the newer types of bombs were a little late in coming?

The Spanish Civil War, which opened in the summer of 1936 and continued until the spring of 1939, provided the *Luftwaffe* with an invaluable opportunity to gain combat experience and test and improve its equipment. The Germans were committed from the very start, following a request by General Franco for aircraft to shift forces loyal to him from North Africa into Spain. Hitler immediately loaned a force of twenty Ju 52's. These aircraft achieved a significance far beyond their meagre number; each one carried some twenty-five men and their equipment the 130 miles from Tetuan to Seville on each sortie, and by flying up to four sorties per day the transports enabled Franco to consolidate his shaky position in the early days of the revolt. The number of German combat aircraft in Spain swelled steadily and by November 1936 the force, now designated the Condor Legion, comprised some two hundred machines; one half of these were Ju 52's operating as bombers and He 51 fighters, while the remainder were ground attack, reconnaissance and transport types. At first the Condor Legion was able to do little, because the He 51 proved to be an inferior fighting machine to the Russian-built I-16 used by the Republicans, and without proper escorts the Ju 52 bomber units were badly knocked about. But in the summer of 1937 the modern Bf 109 fighter and He 111 and Do 17 bombers appeared in action in Spain, and with these machines the Germans rapidly gained the upper hand.

One development which was to do much to shape future German policy was the use of the He 51 in Spain as a fighter bomber, in the close support role with six 22 lb bombs. Flying in formations of nine at low level, the Heinkels were used to hit targets right in front of the ground forces; operating from airfields close to the front line, they would make as many as seven sorties a day. Oberst Wolfram Baron von Richthofen,* the Chief of Staff of the Condor Legion, brought these tactics to a fine peak of efficiency, and the new methods proved decisive during the small scale actions then being fought. A few years

* Cousin of the famous First World War fighter ace.

later, these same tactics were to prove just as effective against bigger opponents.

In spite of a few deficiencies, the eve of the Second World War found the *Luftwaffe* far better prepared for action than any other air force in the world. Its equipment was, by the standards of the day, excellent. The Messerschmitt 109E was superior as an interceptor fighter to anything then in service with the sole exception of the Spitfire, and only a few of the latter were then available. Similarly, the Heinkel 111 and the Junkers 88 were far better than any European bomber in service except for the Wellington, which again existed only in small numbers at that time; that the Germans had no modern four engined bomber in service mattered little then, for neither did any of their opponents.

In terms of training and fighting spirit, too, the men of the *Luftwaffe* were as good as any, and far better than most, of those in the opposing air forces. If war came in Europe there could be little doubt that this newest air force would give a good account of itself. And so it proved.

CHAPTER TWO

On The Offensive

*I have done my best during the past few years to make our air force the
largest and most powerful in the world. The creation of the Greater German
Reich has been made possible largely by the strength and constant readiness
of the air force. Born of the spirit of the German airmen in the First World
War, inspired by its faith in our* Fuehrer *and Commander in Chief—thus
stands the German air force today, ready to carry out every command of the*
Fuehrer *with lightning speed and undreamed-of might.*

Order of the Day from Goering to the Luftwaffe, *August 1939*

THE GERMAN attack on Poland, and with it the Second World War, opened
at a quarter to five on the morning of September 1st, 1939. Fog during the
morning delayed air operations, but by the afternoon the *Luftwaffe* was heavily
committed. *Luftflotten* I and IV, commanded by General Kesselring and
General Loehr respectively, concentrated some 1,300 first-line aircraft against
the Poles. At first the main targets were the airfields, and German bombers
attacked those at Kattowitz, Cracow, Lwow and Radom, Lublin, Wilna, Kida,
Grodno and Warsaw. Even when the out-dated Polish PZL fighters did
manage to get off the ground to intercept, the escorting Messerschmitt 109's
and 110's had little difficulty in fending them off.

From September 3rd the *Luftwaffe* shifted part of its effort away from the
airfields, to operations in support of the army. This co-operation took the
form of direct support in the bombing and strafing of strongpoints, artillery
batteries and concentrations whenever the Poles sought to make a stand. To
dislocate the enemy supply organisation, the bombers attacked depots, dumps,
barracks and factories. Rear lines of communication—railways, stations,
bridges and road junctions—were also attacked, with the object of preventing
the Poles from bringing up fresh reinforcements to the battle areas.

By September 17th the end of the campaign was already in sight, for the
Polish army was no longer operating as a co-ordinated force and the fall of the
capital, Warsaw, was imminent. It was on this day that the Germans began
to move the first units west, to bolster the weak forces left to defend that front
against the British and the French. But in the event the capture of Warsaw
proved to be more difficult than expected, and the Russian invasion of Eastern

Poland gave new impetus to the German endeavours. Throughout the week that followed the *Luftwaffe* dropped many thousands of leaflets on the fortress capital, calling upon the commander, General Blaskowitz, to surrender. When these tactics failed the Germans launched a powerful air and artillery bombardment on the city, on September 25th. General von Richthofen had available some 400 bombers of all types, some of which flew as many as four sorties that day; when night fell Warsaw blazed from end to end. The next day the Polish forces in the capital offered their surrender, and on the 27th the campaign came to an end.

With little or no opposition to hamper them, the German Ju 87 dive bombers had been an outstanding success during the Polish campaign. The pilots were able to exploit the very high inherent accuracy of the steep diving attack to the full. The effect of this almost individual form of combat was devastating to the morale of enemy ground troops unprepared for it; the *Stuka* * legend was born.

Following the victorious autumn campaign in Poland, the *Luftwaffe* units involved withdrew to their bases in Germany to rest and refit; for both the Germans and their enemies in the west this was a time for preparation for the coming summer's campaigns—the so-called 'phoney war'.

Air actions during this period were few and far between. One battle that was notable for its long-term effects was fought on December 18th, 1939. On that day a formation of twenty-two Wellingtons of the R.A.F. attempted a daylight attack on German warships near Wilhelmshaven. At that time there was a popular belief that bombers, heavily armed with large numbers of turreted machine guns and flying in tight formations, would be able to fight their way through an enemy's defences and penetrate to targets in broad daylight. Now the theory was put to the test. When near the north coast of Germany the formation was pounced upon by sixteen Bf 109's and thirty-four Bf 110's. In the brisk and bloody engagement that followed both sides traded blows. Many of the German fighters suffered damage, but only two were shot down; in return, the explosive shells from their heavier calibre cannon had caused fearful damage to the bombers. Of the twenty-two Wellingtons involved in the fight ten were shot down, and two more crash-landed after regaining the coast of England. So it was that the R.A.F. learnt the hard way, as the *Luftwaffe* was to learn in 1940 and the Americans were to learn in 1943, that formations of bombers unescorted by fighters could not survive in daylight in the face of a well-equipped and determined fighter opposition. From then until the autumn of 1944, R.A.F. Bomber Command confined itself almost entirely to night attacks when striking at targets in Germany.

While the ground troops of both sides settled down to the boredom of the

* Although the word '*Stuka*' is often used as the name of the Ju 87, it is in fact a contraction of the German word *Sturzkampfflugzeug*, meaning 'dive bomber'. Thus the term '*Stuka*' describes all dive bombers and not any particular one.

'phoney war', the German planning staffs were far from idle. The main effort for 1940 was to be the offensive in France and the Low Countries in the late spring. But first Hitler demanded the capture of Denmark and Norway to, as he put it, 'anticipate English action against Scandinavia and the Baltic'.

Exercise Weser,* as the attacks on Denmark and Norway were code-named, opened on April 9th. Land forces crossed the Danish frontier, while simultaneously seaborne forces landed on the Danish islands and at the Norwegian ports. Air transport operations began one and a half hours later with paratroop † drops—the first parachute assault landing ever—at the two airfields at Aalborg. With the airfields secure, Ju 52's landed with the infantry of the consolidating force. Soon Aalborg itself, together with the whole of Jutland and Copenhagen, was in German hands. Demonstrations of bomber and fighter units, combined with a massed fly-past by transport aircraft bound for Norway, served to convince the Danes that further resistance was futile, and before the end of the day the King ordered his troops to cease fire.

Meanwhile, in Norway, the seaborne landings at the ports had been followed by fighter attacks on the airfields at Stavanger and Oslo. The small Norwegian fighter force, its equipment out-dated, was all but wiped out. These operations were immediately followed by paratroop drops and air-landed reinforcements on the two airfields, which were soon in German hands. Within a short time Bf 110's and Ju 87's were operating from there in support of the German ground forces, and after two days the German lodgement area contained the airfields at Stavanger and Trondheim as well.

Throughout these operations the Germans made the fullest use of air transport to move in troops and *Luftwaffe* ground crewmen; five hundred Ju 52's were available, one-third of them from the so-called 'bomber *Gruppen* for special employment',‡ the remainder from the advanced flying training schools. Now, for the first time, the German peacetime theories on air transport operations were put to the test during a large scale action. They were not found wanting.

By the time the first British troops landed in Norway, at Narvik, Namsos and Andalsnes, on April 15th, 16th and 17th respectively, the area occupied by the Germans in the south had already been secured and extended. Now the main effort of *Fliegerkorps* X, the *Luftwaffe* formation concerned, was directed against the British landing points and the sea transports and their naval escorts. Heavy and dive-bomber units kept up a steady pressure and, in the face of negligible air opposition, caused serious damage. At the peak of their strength,

* *Weseruebung.*

† Unlike the British and American airborne armies which followed them, the German paratroops belonged to the air force. They were part of 7 *Flieger Division.*

‡ *Kampfgruppe zur besonderen Verwendung.* This designation was given to the transport units as a sop to morale, so that aircrewmen flying with them would not feel that their task was one of only secondary importance. In 1943, when the transport crews had won their spurs in action and this psychological prop was no longer needed, the units were redesignated *Transport Gruppen.*

at the beginning of May, the *Fliegerkorps* X units in Norway comprised the following:

Long range bombers (He 111, Ju 88)	360
Dive bombers (Ju 87)	50
Single engined fighters (Bf 109)	50
Twin engined fighters (Bf 110)	70
Reconnaissance (Do 17)	60
Coastal types (He 115, He 59, Do 18)	120
	710

In the face of such opposition the R.A.F. found it almost impossible to build up its forces. An attempt to operate out-dated Gladiator fighters from frozen lakes was soon spotted by German reconnaissance aircraft, and the landing surfaces were quickly made useless by bombing. Only at the very end of the campaign were a few Hurricanes made available, but these too were able to do little.

The German army moved relentlessly northwards up the length of Norway, and early in May the British and French forces which had been fighting in the south at Andalsnes and Namsos were evacuated; the main centre of resistance left was now in the north at Narvik. A month later the troops there were withdrawn as well, and on June 10th the campaign ended with the Germans in possession of the whole of Norway.

The special significance of the Norwegian campaign was that from first to last the *Luftwaffe* proved to be a decisive factor in its success. As we have seen, the rapid occupation of Oslo and Stavanger was made possible only by the use of paratroops and air-landed units, while the air force had intervened decisively in the ground fighting in an area where communications were poor and usually dependent upon a single road running through a valley. By and large, the operations in Norway served as a very useful dress rehearsal for the much larger offensive due to open soon after, in Flanders.

Boldness had long been a feature of German military planning, and the projected drive through France in 1940 was certainly no exception. In contrast to the relatively small encircling movements during the Polish campaign, an immensely powerful armoured spearhead was now to punch straight through the French defences on a narrow front, and push its way to the north-west to the coast more than two hundred miles away. If it succeeded, the plan would cut the Allied ground forces into two halves, which could then be dealt with individually. The move would carry with it a certain element of risk, but with powerful and direct air support by the most concentrated air forces yet employed, a form of moving artillery barrage could prepare the way with a degree of surprise and mobility not possible with conventional artillery. Provided that the enemy could be kept under constant pressure, and allowed no pause for recovery, there was every chance that the plan would succeed. So far as the plan for the air support went, it was really only the large scale practical application of the lessons learnt in Spain and improved in Poland. Now von Richthofen's dive bombers had proved their worth, and they were to be given the chance to take a decisive part in the battle.

But before the campaign in France opened, the German High Command felt it necessary to secure its northern flank in Holland and Belgium. It was expected that the Dutch would attempt to stop the Germans along the lines of the Maas and Yssel rivers then, if these were crossed, in Rotterdam itself. In the case of Belgium the defences were concentrated on the Meuse River and the Albert Canal, and the whole line hinged on the massively constructed Fort Eben Émael where the two met. To seize vital bridges in the path of the advancing armour the Germans planned to use airborne troops as in Norway and Denmark, but on a far greater scale. Fort Eben Emael itself was to be taken in a *coup de main* by troops landed in the compound in an entirely novel way: by means of troop-carrying gliders.

Thus the *Luftwaffe* was to play a threefold role during the campaign. First, it was to clear the way for the airborne operations by powerful attacks on enemy airfields. Secondly, it was to transport the airborne troops to their objectives. Third, it was to support the German armies during the operations to take Holland and Belgium, and later during the projected armoured thrust into France itself. The aircraft available for the undertaking were approximately as follows:

Long range bombers	1,300
Dive bombers	380
Single engined fighters	860
Twin engined fighters	350
Reconnaissance	640
Transport aircraft	475
Assault gliders	45
	4,050

The German attack on the airfields in Holland and Belgium, as well as those used by the British and French air forces in France, opened at first light on May 10th, 1940. On the very first day the Germans secured air superiority, and never lost it. Then the Ju 52's went in with their loads of paratroopers. At The Hague the three main airfields were taken almost immediately, as was the important Moerdijk bridge near Rotterdam; however, the planned attempt to capture the Dutch Royal Family and government failed.

In Belgium the attacks by glider-borne troops on the bridges over the Maas near Maastricht, and on the Fort Eben Emael, succeeded brilliantly. In the case of the attack on the fort, just 85 German assault pioneers succeeded in neutralising the complex underground system of fortifications manned by 750 Belgian soldiers, until German reinforcements arrived and the garrison surrendered. Of the German force six men were killed and fifteen were wounded; such was the power of surprise. Now the way was open for the German armoured units to plunge deeply into Holland and Belgium and, according to plan, the defenders were not allowed any breathing space. Five days later, on May 15th, the Dutch capitulated.

During the invasions of Holland and Belgium the *Luftwaffe* reconnaissance units had been busy reporting on the dispositions of the British and French forces, and the German High Command thus had an accurate and up-to-date picture of their strengths and weaknesses.

It was at 4 p.m. on May 13th that the aerial 'softening up' of the French positions on the west bank of the Meuse began. Wave after wave of dive and horizontal bombers pounded the defenders' positions, and before nightfall the *Luftwaffe* had mounted more than 500 sorties. Under their cover General Heinz Guderian's 1st *Panzer* Division crossed the Meuse and, after bringing up its armour over a hastily constructed pontoon bridge, punched its way through the main and secondary lines of the French defences.

The forcing of the Meuse proved to be the decisive turning point of the campaign, for once the German armoured thrust to the coast got under way nothing the British or the French could do could stop it. Operating under strong fighter escort, von Richthofen's dive bombers were called in time and time again to prepare a way for the tanks. Immediately air or ground reconnaissance detected actual or likely points of resistance the dive bombers, which frequently flew as many as nine sorties per day per aircraft, would concentrate to neutralise it. The net result was a paralysation of the British and French armies that was a revelation to the Germans themselves.

On the evening of May 20th, just one week and 240 miles after the German tanks had set out across the Meuse, the spearhead of the thrust reached the English Channel at Voyelles. The German plan had worked: the British and French armies were cut neatly in two. It was the beginning of the end of the Battle of France.

In the meantime, however, the pace of the advance had presented the *Luftwaffe* with the problem of maintaining ever-lengthening lines of supply. The single engined fighter, dive bomber and short range reconnaissance units were forced to move their bases almost daily. In their support, the Ju 52's of the versatile transport force operated continuously to supply their needs.

By May 30th the position of the British and French forces cut off in northern France had become untenable, and the evacuation from Dunkirk began. Immediately Goering ordered the *Luftwaffe* to concentrate its fighters and bombers over the port, in an effort to prevent the withdrawal. But for the short range units, operating after the cumulative wear and tear of three weeks of intensive operations, from recently captured airfields on the end of tenuous lines of supply, there was a wide gap between what Goering wanted and what was possible. Moreover, the German formations often found their way to the evacuation beaches barred by R.A.F. fighters operating from bases in southern England. For the first time the *Luftwaffe* met an opponent of equal fighting capabilities, in the air and in force; the result was that the German bombers, and in particular the dive bombers, suffered heavily. The evacuation from Dunkirk was not stopped; when it came to an end on the morning of June 4th, a total of 338,226 men had been snatched back to England.

After the evacuation of Dunkirk the *Luftwaffe*, freed of its commitment in the north, turned its attention to the next objective: the support of the army as it struck towards Paris. Within ten days the French capital had fallen; eleven days later, on June 25th, the French sued for peace. The campaign in the west was over, just forty-six breathtaking days after it had opened.

Few would blame the Germans for the feeling of euphoria that swept over them at this time. They had succeeded beyond all but their wildest dreams. But it is a truism of war that one learns far more from one's defeats than one ever does from victories. The first brushes with the R.A.F. had been, for the most part, inconclusive, and in their flush of victory few Germans realised their wider implications.

When the German General Staff came to consider the invasion of the final and most troublesome enemy, Britain, it is hardly surprising that the problem came to be treated in the same way as the crossing of the Meuse, only on a far larger scale. As before, the *Luftwaffe* was to take the place of the artillery. But first the Germans would need air supremacy. Goering accepted that the R.A.F., as the most powerful single air force yet encountered, would take longer to subdue than the one or two days which had been sufficient in the past; it might perhaps take his men as long as two weeks to complete its destruction.

During July German fighter and bomber units concentrated in *Luftflotten* 2 and 3 along the Channel coast, and by the 17th of the month the Order of Battle was as follows:

Long range bombers	1,200
Dive bombers	280
Single engined fighters	760
Twin engined fighters	220
Reconnaissance aircraft	140
	2,600

In addition were the forces of *Luftflotte* 5 bases in Norway, with the range to intervene in the battle over Britain. These amounted to

Long range bombers	130
Twin engined fighters	30
Reconnaissance aircraft	30
	190

The initial task of the *Luftwaffe* during the forthcoming operations was to be a twofold one: first, it was to eliminate the R.A.F. as an effective fighting force; second, it was to strangle Britain's maritime lifeline by attacks on ports and shipping.

The action now known as the Battle of Britain opened in earnest on August 13th, with 485 bomber and 1,000 fighter sorties by the *Luftwaffe* against Portland and Southampton, and also airfields in Hampshire and Kent. When the day ended the Germans had lost 45 aircraft, the R.A.F., 13. Two days later the *Luftwaffe* struck again in even greater force: with 1,786 sorties, 520 of them by bombers, it endeavoured to knock out the British airfields. The R.A.F. fought back vigorously, and shot down 75 of the raiders for a loss of 34 fighters. However, the German effort was repeated again on the 16th, with a loss of 16 aircraft, and on the 18th with a loss of 71.

This pace of operations continued throughout the rest of August and early September. Gradually the realisation permeated through the ranks of the German air force, from the bottom to the top, that this battle was not going to be easily won—if indeed it was going to be won at all. Adolf Galland, who at the time commanded the Third *Gruppe* of J.G. 26 with Bf 109's, later wrote:*

'Failure to achieve any noticeable success, constantly changing orders betraying lack of purpose and obvious misjudgment of the situation by the Command, and unjustified accusations had a most demoralising effect on us fighter pilots, who were already overtaxed by physical and mental strain. We complained of the leadership, the bombers, the *Stukas*, and were dissatisfied with ourselves. We saw one comrade after another, old and tested brothers in combat, vanish from our ranks. Not a day passed without a place remaining empty at the mess table. New faces appeared and became familiar, until one day these too would disappear, shot down in the Battle of Britain.'

What had gone wrong? The fact of the matter was that the *Luftwaffe*, victorious on all fronts up till now, had bitten off more than it could chew.

To win the battle the Germans had to knock out the R.A.F. as a viable fighting force; this could be done either by luring the British fighters into the air and destroying them there, or else by attacking the fighter airfields and destroying them on the ground. Since the German bombers were soon proved to be unable to defend themselves against the British fighters by their own fire, they could penetrate to their targets only under cover of a strong fighter escort; the escorts, then, were to destroy the R.A.F. fighters in the air. But, as soon became clear also, the twin engined Messerschmitt 110's were no match for the more nimble single engined British fighters. That meant that the task of escorting the bombers fell to the single engined Messerschmitt 109, the only German aircraft able to fight on equal terms with the Spitfires and Hurricanes.

* *The First and the Last*, Methuen & Co.

The Bf 109, like its British counterparts, was a short range interceptor with a radius of action of about 125 miles. It could therefore provide an effective escort only as far as London, from the airfields in the Calais area, or to a little past Portsmouth, from airfields in the Cherbourg area. This was the nub of the German problem, for the range of the escorts marked the limit to which the bombers could go in daylight without suffering swingeing losses. The *Luftwaffe* rendered unusable many of the airfields within the range of the Bf 109 but Air Chief Marshal Dowding, the British commander, prudently moved most of his squadrons outside this area and therefore out of effective reach of the bombers.

September saw the battle being fought out over London itself, with the British fighters fighting close to their bases and those of the Germans at near to the limit of their range; the ratio of single seat fighters was only about 7:6 in the Germans' favour, and the British were operating under efficient radar control from the ground and thus able to deploy their force much more effectively. With the British fighter pilots man for man as capable as their German counterparts, and a similar parity in equipment, the issue was not long in doubt.

Given these basic and insurmountable problems, it is clear that whichever way Goering chose to use his force he was unlikely to succeed in the destruction of the R.A.F. In the event he chose to fight a long drawn out battle of attrition which cost him, between July 10th and October 31st, a total of 1,733 aircraft as against 915 British fighters shot down. Even the German air force could not go on suffering such losses for such a poor return, and by November the battle had ground to a halt. It would be left for the Americans to show that a daylight bombing offensive in the face of a powerful defensive system was possible. But that, as we shall see, was with somewhat different equipment and not until much later in the war.

To what extent was the Battle of Britain a turning point in the war? Certainly it did not mark the beginning of the end of the *Luftwaffe*, for that force continued in being and was still to achieve triumphs as great as those secured in France. But what was important was that, for the first time, the main body of the *Luftwaffe* had been brought to bear during a large scale operation lasting several weeks, and had failed to gain its objectives. The myth of the invincibility of the *Luftwaffe* had been exploded.

With the failure of its daylight attack, the *Luftwaffe* shifted the weight of its effort to night attacks on Britain. This had begun on August 28th, when for three consecutive nights strong forces of bombers raided Liverpool. Then, on September 7th, the so-called night *Blitz* * on London opened. Between then

* *Blitz*, short for *Blitzkrieg*—'lightning war'. To the British public the visible manifestation of the German 'lightning war' methods was in the air raids. So it was that the word *Blitz*, the German for 'lightning', came to be incorporated in the English language with the meaning 'bombing attack'.

and November 13th the Germans bombed the British capital almost every night, with an average raiding force of 130 bombers.

During these attacks the bombers would cross the British coast singly, moving on parallel tracks confined to a narrow belt some fifteen miles in breadth. These 'crocodiles' were quite different from the 'stream' tactics employed by R.A.F. Bomber Command later in the war, since the German crews made no attempt to concentrate in time and space. Instead they flew in at intervals of about four minutes, with an average spacing between bombers of twelve miles. This made it very difficult for the 'cat's-eye' fighters * to intercept, for there was only one raider per 180 square miles. Taking into account the altitude dispersion of the bombers between 10,000 and 20,000 feet, there was an average of one aircraft per 345 cubic miles of airspace! Small wonder the defenders, for the most part without the necessary precision radar equipment, were able to achieve little during the dark nights of 1940.

Now the German long range radio beam systems had a chance to prove their worth. The *Luftwaffe* signals organisation had erected nine *Knickebein* transmitting stations along the coasts of France, Holland and Norway, in addition to the three erected in Germany before the war; these transmitters could point out any target in the British Isles with their guiding beams. But in the event *Knickebein* was to prove a failure. During the light night probing attacks immediately after the Dunkirk evacuation German aircraft operating over Britain had made use of the guiding beams to find their way about. The result was that even before the large scale night bombing raids began the British Intelligence service had penetrated the secrets of the German system, and the R.A.F. had time to set up a special organisation to jam out the beams.†

With *Knickebein* effectively nullified, the *Luftwaffe* was forced to make a much greater use of its precision bombing aid *X-Geraet*. The idea evolved that *Kampfgruppe* 100, whose aircraft carried it, should drop incendiary bombs to light fires at the target, to guide other crews in; in this way the beam-flying crews were to act as pathfinders for the rest of the German bomber force.

Kampfgruppe 100 first operated in its new pathfinder role on the night of November 14th, 1940, when the target was Coventry. Fires started by the leading unit guided bombers in from all directions. One 'Crocodile' of attacking bombers came in over the Wash, another over the Isle of Wight, and a third over Brighton. The night was clear and in the moonlight the approaching crews were able to see every detail of the burning city. Altogether 449 bombers hit Coventry during the ten hours of the attack, and between them they dropped 56 tons of incendiaries, 394 tons of high explosive bombs and 127 parachute mines. As a result much of the city centre was reduced to a smoking ruin and

* Fighters not fitted with radar.

† For a full description of the discovery and jamming of *Knickebein*, and also the other German beam and radar systems, see *Instruments of Darkness* by Alfred Price, William Kimber, London.

twenty-one important factories, twelve of them directly concerned with air-craft production, were severely damaged. During the course of the attack some five hundred and fifty people were killed, and a further eight hundred seriously wounded. It was a striking demonstration of what the *Luftwaffe* could do when using a pathfinder force guided to the target by precision radio beams. During the months that followed *Kampfgruppe* 100 led many attacks, but because of the steadily growing barrage of radio jamming put out by the R.A.F. the Coventry success was never repeated.

In the early part of 1941, first in a trickle and then in a flood, the German bomber units moved to the east in preparation for the invasion of Russia. The bombers were scheduled to return to France to renew the night attack on Britain six weeks after the opening of the offensive in the east—a conservative estimate of how long the campaign was expected to last. In the event the force was never to return to France in anything like its original strength.

The move to the east had begun in a small way in January, February and March, as some 400 German aircraft slowly collected in allied Rumania in preparation for the attack on Greece. From the start the Germans had taken it for granted that the Yugoslavs would fall in with their grand design. But when a *coup d'etat* ousted the pro-German government in Yugoslavia on March 27th, Hitler decided to occupy that country as well in order to secure his southern flank.

To reinforce *Luftflotte* 4 in the Balkans to enable it to cover the attack on Yugoslavia as well as Greece, a further 600 combat aircraft were transferred from the west. That such a large force was able to move to bases one thousand miles away from those previously occupied in France, and operate at half of its established strength within ten days of the order to move, illustrates once again the impressive mobility of the *Luftwaffe*. The force had received a bloody nose from the R.A.F. over Britain, but it was still more than a match for any other air force in Europe.

On April 6th, Palm Sunday, the Germans struck in the Balkans. The *Luftwaffe* opened its assault on Yugoslavia with a saturation bombing attack on the capital, Belgrade, early that morning. Flying in relays from airfields in Austria and Rumania, 150 bombers and dive bombers with a strong fighter escort went in to attack. The initial raid was carried out in three distinct waves at fifteen minute intervals, and each wave bombed for about twenty min-utes. Thus Belgrade was subjected to a continuous rain of bombs for almost one and a half hours. The first wave wiped out the weak Yugoslav Air Force and the anti-aircraft gun defences, with the result that the dive bombers could go down as low as they liked to make sure of hitting their targets: the principal government buildings and the centre of the capital. When the attack on the ill-prepared city closed, seventeen thousand people lay dead in its ruins. Having thus delivered the knock-out blow on the capital, the dive bombers were able to shift their efforts to their more usual targets: lines of communications, troop concentrations, and the close support of ground operations. As in the past the combination of aerial preparation and armoured thrusts proved irresistible, and within twelve days the Yugoslavs had capitulated.

No less successful was the attack on Greece. On the very first evening a lucky bomb struck the ammunition ship *Clan Frazer* at Pireaus, and the 250 tons of explosive in her holds went off in an explosion which wrecked the port from end to end. The explosion was, in the words of the British fleet commander, Admiral Cunningham, 'A shattering blow'. At one stroke it deprived the British of the one reasonably equipped base in Greece through which supplies could be passed to the armies there. Thus handicapped, the weak British and Greek forces could fight little more than a delaying action, and by April 28th the whole of the mainland was in German hands. Only the strategically placed island of Crete, some sixty miles away to the south, remained.

It was Generaloberst Kurt Student, the commander of the German airborne forces, who first put forward the idea of an airborne invasion of the island. He pointed out to Goering that the island could be a useful stepping stone for any future attack on Cyprus or the Suez Canal. Goering liked the idea, and obtained Hitler's permission. The attack on Crete was to be entirely a *Luftwaffe* matter, and the German Army General Staff was not consulted.

For the operation a force of 530 Ju 52's and 100 assault gliders assembled at airfields in the Athens area, with a further 650 fighter, bomber and reconnaissance aircraft at bases within easy range of Crete. Prior to the attack the German bombers systematically knocked out each of the British airfields on the island. Now the stage was set.

The airborne assault on Crete, Operation Mercury,* opened early on the morning of May 20th. After an intensive 'softening up' operation by He 111's, Do 17's and Ju 87's, which lasted an hour, the first waves of parachute and glider-borne troops landed at Malme, Canea, Retina and Heraklion. At first things went very badly indeed for the Germans, and the airborne units suffered heavy casualties. But in the face of continuous and heavy air attacks the British Commonwealth troops were forced to give ground. Once the Germans had secured the airfield at Malme, Ju 52's poured in with fresh troops as well as supplies, while the unchallenged *Luftwaffe* prevented their enemies from receiving worthwhile quantities of either. On May 27th General Wavell informed Mr Churchill 'I fear we must recognise that Crete is no longer tenable . . .' On the next day the evacuation of the island began.

Throughout the battle for Crete the Royal Navy had braved the dive bombers and turned back almost all the German attempts to bring in reinforcements by sea; now, at no less heavy cost, it took off more than sixteen thousand weary Commonwealth troops before the final surrender on June 1st. The cost to the British fleet was grievously heavy: three cruisers and six destroyers were

* *Einsatz Merkur.*

sunk; three battleships, one aircraft carrier, seven cruisers and four destroyers were damaged.

But the German airborne troops had suffered heavily as well: out of 13,000 men engaged, some 4,500 had been killed or were listed as missing. Moreover, 271 Ju 52 transports were destroyed or damaged beyond repair, just over half of those committed. Never again would the Germans mount a large scale airborne assault, for Crete had become, in the words of Generaloberst Student 'the grave of the German paratroops'.

Throughout 1941 and 1942 the *Luftwaffe* maintained a steady pressure on Malta, and the irregular attempts by the British to push supply convoys through to the island invariably resulted in large scale battles. The Germans and the Italians seriously considered an airborne invasion of the island during 1942, but the spectre of large scale losses as in Crete loomed large, and the plan came to nothing. As a result Malta remained, strong and defiant, and whenever the Germans ceased their aerial bombardment she became a sharp thorn in the German and Italian sides; aircraft and submarines operating from the island took a steady toll of the supplies intended for the Axis forces in North Africa.

Hitler's decision to invade Russia had aroused grave misgivings amongst the officers of the German General Staff, who saw clearly that the resultant war on two fronts might well prove to be beyond their nation's capabilities. Goering tried hard to turn Hitler from this course, but the latter, convinced that the Russians were themselves preparing for an aggressive war against Germany, refused to be swayed.

The German preparations for the attack on Russia had begun as early as October 1940, even before the daylight air attacks on Britain had finally come to an end. From then until the spring of 1941 airfield construction units of the *Luftwaffe* had set about the task of improving the airfields in occupied Poland. In March 1941, as the weather improved, this programme was accelerated. In the interests of security the majority of the flying units were held back in the west or in Germany until the beginning of June. Then, within a space of three weeks, the remainder of the aircraft allocated to the operation moved swiftly and secretly into the bases prepared for them. *Luftflotte* 5 was to cover the northern part of the front, *Luftflotte* 1 the centre and *Luftflotte* 4 the southern part; the breakdown of the force was as follows:

Long range bombers	775
Dive bombers	310
Single engined fighters	830
Twin engined fighters	90
Reconnaissance	710
Coastal types	55
	2,770

When the attack opened before dawn on June 22nd, 1941, the previous German security measures paid handsome dividends. The Russians were taken by complete surprise. As in the past, the first priority of the *Luftwaffe* was the elimination of the opposing air force; Soviet aircraft were destroyed by the hundred as they sat out in neat rows on their airfields. The official Soviet postwar publication *History of the Great Patriotic War of the Soviet Union* gives details of the magnitude of the blow suffered:

'During the first days of the war enemy bomber formations launched massive attacks on sixty-six airfields of the frontier region, above all on those where new types of Soviet fighters were based. The result of these raids and of the violent air-to-air battles was a loss to us, as at noon on June 22nd, of some 1,200 aircraft, including more than 800 destroyed on the ground.'

With the Soviet air force now unable to intervene with any effect, the *Luftwaffe* was able to concentrate almost its entire effort to the support of the army. The tried and tested methods of concentrating all available bombing aircraft—long range as well as dive bombers—against enemy communications, troop concentrations and even close support targets, was repeated after the pattern established in Poland and France. As in the past, the rapid advance of the German army through Soviet occupied Poland and western Russia demanded the greatest mobility on the part of the close support forces; once again the *Luftwaffe* ground organisation proved equal to the task.

One of the outstanding features of the early part of this campaign was the lavish use made of aerial reconnaissance; we have already seen that more than a quarter of the German aircraft involved were reconnaissance types. The *Luftwaffe* was able to give the army commanders a detailed and up-to-date picture of enemy dispositions and movements both in the fighting zones and in the rear areas—an advantage that often proved decisive in a campaign where rapid movement was the order of the day.

In spite of the fact that nearly half the operational strength of the *Luftwaffe* was concentrated in Russia during the initial stages of the attack, the enormous width of the front—over one thousand miles—meant that the Germans could not be strong everywhere at once. Close support units had therefore to move rapidly from one part of the front to another in order to support the attacks wherever the army high command gave each successive priority.

Throughout the summer and autumn of 1941 the German advance continued unchecked. Brest Litovsk, Minsk, Smolensk and Kiev all fell in quick succession following great encircling pincer movements. However these victories were not always bought cheaply, and the German method of using all types of bomber for close support work had serious disadvantages. The *Luftwaffe* learnt to its cost that the Russian army habit of firing at enemy aircraft with any weapon that came to hand did, over a long period, cause serious losses. The losses of cheaper aircraft—dive bombers and army co-operation types—were bad enough, but the steady drain on the more expensive He 111's and Ju 88's was such that replacements failed to keep pace with losses. Gradually, and hardly perceptibly at first, the fighting strength of the *Luftwaffe* was draining away.

When the weather broke at the end of October, and their armoured thrusts slithered to a halt in axle-deep mud, the Germans had surrounded Leningrad and were at the gates of Moscow itself. But Generals 'Mud' and 'Winter' had struck before the Germans had gained the total victory so confidently predicted by Hitler. The severity of the Russian winter caught the German army and air force ill prepared. Apart from the lack of proper clothing and accommodation, the latter was also without the necessary equipment to maintain its aircraft in the open under such conditions; in temperatures of minus 20° F— 52 degrees of frost—aero engines and machine guns simply froze solid. The net result was that the serviceability in the already weakened flying units fell to as low as thirty per cent. The *Luftwaffe* desperately needed a breathing space to settle down to its new environment, and to rest and re-equip units depleted during the exertions of the period of intensive operations. But they were not to get one, for on December 5th the Russians launched their own counter-offensive.

The initial success of the Russian attacks, which at one time threatened the entire German front with collapse, forced the *Luftwaffe* units to continue operating under the most trying circumstances. In many cases the only way to provide any worthwhile relief to the hard pressed ground forces was to send every combat aircraft that would fly, whether it was fully serviceable or not, into action in the threatened areas. Nevertheless the Russians did make some useful gains; and at Demyansk, a small town almost mid-way between Moscow and Leningrad, they succeeded in cutting off six German divisions totalling approximately one hundred thousand men. To continue fighting effectively, such a force needed just under 300 tons of supplies per day. It was decided that the *Luftwaffe* would fly them in.

The airlift into Demyansk, the first large scale airlift operation ever, opened on February 20th, 1942 when forty heavily laden Ju 52's flew into the pocket, unloaded, and returned with wounded. The distance from the nearest airhead to the pocket, at Pleskau, was 150 miles, one hundred of which were over enemy territory. At first the German transports flew in singly at low level, but as the Russian anti-aircraft fire and the fighters became more troublesome they took to going in formations of between twenty and forty at 6,000 feet, with a fighter escort. What had started off as a temporary expedient soon developed into a protracted operation, for it was not until May 18th that the siege could be lifted. By dint of pulling in Ju 52's from every possible source— including the instrument flying training schools in Germany—the *Luftwaffe* did manage to move in an average of just over 300 tons of supplies per day. But it was a close run thing, and the need to put together a force of six hundred serviceable transport aircraft for the operation clearly extended the *Luftwaffe* to the very utmost; from start to finish the operation cost 265 aircraft destroyed or damaged beyond repair. As we shall soon see, the success at Demyansk was to create a very dangerous precedent.

The Russians kept up their pressure until early in April 1942, when the thaw set in and the resultant mud again brought operations to a halt. When the summer came it was the Germans who were again in their element, and now they launched their offensive. The goal for 1942 was to be the rich oilfields of the Caucasus; but first, in order to secure their southern flank, the Germans needed to complete the capture of the Crimea—and in particular the fortress at Sevastopol.

The hard-hitting *Fliegerkorps VIII*, commanded by Generaloberst von Richthofen, now comprised some 600 aircraft; these included three *Gruppen* of dive bombers, seven of heavy bombers, and four *Gruppen* of fighters. In the past this formation had been sent to support the most critical operations, in view of its proven ability to provide close air support on the very heaviest scale. Accordingly, in May 1942, the unit was shifted from the Central to the Southern front.

Richthofen believed that he could best support the army's attack on Sevastopol by breaking the morale of the Russian defenders. So the Soviet troops in the area were kept under extreme pressure from the air, at the same time as the German army subjected them to a heavy artillery bombardment. The assault on Sevastopol began on June 2nd, and continued until Russian resistance in the fortress finally ended on July 4th. During the battle Major Werner Baumbach flew as commander of *Kampfgeschwader* 30; one may form an impression of the intensity of the air operations from his diary written at the time: *

'From the air Sevastopol looked like a painter's battle panorama. In the early morning the sky swarmed with aircraft hurrying to unload their bombs on the town. Thousands of bombs—more than 2,400 tons of high explosive and 23,000 incendiaries—were dropped on the town and fortress. A single sortie took no more than twenty minutes. By the time you had gained the necessary altitude you were in the target area . . . The Russian A.A. was silenced in the first few days so the danger to aircraft was less than in attacks on the Caucasus harbours or Russian airfields. Yet our work at Sevastopol made the highest demands on men and material. Twelve, fourteen and even up to eighteen sorties were made daily by individual crews. A Ju 88 with fuel tanks full made three or four sorties without the crew stretching their legs.'

Meanwhile the Germans had gone on to the offensive in North Africa as
* *Broken Swastika*, published by Robert Hale.

well. In the spring of 1942 the strength of the *Luftwaffe* in the area had risen to 260 aircraft; with Italian units the force available was some 600 aircraft strong. On May 26th, 1942 the German *Afrika Korps*, with strong air support, thrust eastwards against the British line at Gazala. General Erwin Rommel, the German ground commander, decided to outflank the British line and its southern pivot, at Bir Hakeim, became the focal point of the battle. By making a total of 1,400 sorties against the strongpoint the *Luftwaffe* made a sizeable contribution to its fall on June 11th. Once past the Gazala line Rommel maintained his momentum, and by again bringing large scale air support to bear, the Germans captured the British fortress at Tobruk on June 20th.

But for the rest of the German advance to Alamein the *Luftwaffe* was able to do little, for the stocks of aviation fuel carefully accumulated during the previous months had been exhausted. During the summer of 1942 the British air-sea blockade of North Africa slowed Axis supplies to a mere trickle, with the result that the *Luftwaffe* became less and less effective while the R.A.F. in Egypt became stronger with each day that passed.

When the British launched their own offensive at Alamein on October 24th, 1942, they enjoyed almost complete air superiority. The German retreat never did become a route, but by the time it ended early in 1943 they had been expelled from Egypt and Libya, and were fighting hard to retain a foothold in Tunisia.

Along the Channel coast what had been a holding campaign for the Germans slowly became a major theatre of operations, as the Western Allies slowly gained the initiative in the air. The R.A.F. night bombing offensive had steadily gained in strength, with the introduction of the new four engined Stirlings, Halifaxes and Lancasters into large scale service during 1942.

To parry this air assault on the German cities was General Joseph Kammhuber's night fighter organisation. At the end of September 1942 this force was equipped with some 350 twin engined fighters, for the most part radar-equipped Bf 110's. The fighters themselves were directed to within radar range of their targets by ground controllers using more powerful sets. A line of fighter control stations, one station every twenty miles, formed a barrier through which the attackers had to pass. The barrier was shaped like a giant sickle: the 'handle' ran through Denmark from north to south, and the 'blade' curved through northern Germany, Holland, Belgium and eastern France to the Swiss frontier. Each fighter control radar station had an effective radar range of thirty miles, and the method of control bore the code-name *Himmelbett.** As more and more stations became operational in front and behind the original line, the system began to take a serious toll of the attackers.

In addition to the night fighters, the *Luftwaffe* controlled the anti-aircraft guns which defended the targets now being attacked. By the summer of 1942 there

* Four-poster bed.

were more than 12,000 heavy guns—88 mm., 105 mm. and 128 mm.—allocated to the defence of Germany and the occupied territories in the west.

A further disturbing development for the Germans was the beginning of the American daylight bombing attacks, in August 1942, though at first these were confined to targets in France, Holland and Belgium. In the beginning the German fighter pilots regarded the heavily armed B-17's with considerable apprehension, and at first they were loth to press home their attacks. But it soon became clear that the effect of the bombers' guns was more psychological than material, and the fighter pilots soon regained their old aggressive spirit. Major Egon Meyer of J.G. 2 developed a method of attacking the B-17's from the front, where they were less heavily armed, and by using these tactics the German successes mounted.

With their southern flank secure following the capture of the Crimea in the summer of 1942, the Germans were able to push ahead with their plan to thrust for the Caucasus oilfields in southern Russia. The main offensive began on June 28th, with a breakthrough near Kursk. By July 6th the German army had reached the River Don at Voronezh, and now it wheeled south-eastwards. Once again the *Luftwaffe* was able to demonstrate its old prowess, and provide excellent support for the rapidly advancing armoured units. By August 10th the leading troops were already deep in the Caucasus, more than 300 miles from the starting point. And on the eastern flank German patrols reached the outskirts of the city that was soon to be the scene of one of the bloodiest battles of the war: Stalingrad.

Perhaps if Tsaritsyn had not been renamed Stalingrad in 1925,* the city might not have acted as a magnet for the opposing forces. For certainly the strategic importance of that industrial centre named after the Russian dictator was not so great that it justified a fight to the death between two great nations. But whatever the reason, it was there that both Hitler and Stalin concentrated their forces in August 1942. By November the battle was still in progress as the two opposing armies, each comprising more than a million men and each supported by an air force numbering over a thousand aircraft, fought out a slugging match on a scale unique in the Second World War. With their usual intensive close air support from the *Luftwaffe*, the German troops smashed their way deeper and deeper into the city, until by November 18th they were in possession of almost the entire west bank of the Volga. Now the Russians struck back.

On November 19th the Russian army groups holding the line to the north and to the south of Stalingrad sliced through the weak forces opposing them, and advanced swiftly towards each other. On the afternoon of the 24th the two claws of the pincers met, to enclose twenty-two German divisions comprising 330,000 men inside the pocket. At this stage the Russians had still to con-

* Following the denunciation of Stalin, the city was renamed yet again, Volgagrad, in 1961.

solidate their gains, and there is little doubt that the trapped German troops could have broken out of the cordon—albeit with the loss of much of their heavy equipment. Hitler asked Goering whether the *Luftwaffe* could keep the army at Stalingrad supplied as it had done at Demyansk; the latter, ever reluctant to admit that anything was beyond his force, said that the job could be done. Even when he had had time to re-consider what he had said, and knew that the task was hardly possible, the proud Goering would not go back on what he had told Hitler. The die was cast.

Basing his orders on Goering's promise, Hitler told Generaloberst Paulus, the commander of the forces besieged in Stalingrad, to stand fast and wait for the *Luftwaffe* to fly in the necessary supplies. But now the magnitude of the task became clear to the air staff officers charged with planning the operation, for Paulus' supply requirement amounted to an absolute minimum of 500 tons per day. Since the forces in the pocket were severed from even their own forward supply depots there was little food stored inside the fortress, and the army was living almost from hand to mouth. It was vital that the airlift be started with the utmost urgency.

The regular transport units began operations with their Ju 52's almost immediately, as each aircraft carried two tons of supplies into the pocket each sortie. Meanwhile, the *Luftwaffe* Quartermaster General and his staff ran a fine-toothed comb through the entire air force, searching for any machines capable of taking part in the airlift. By the beginning of December 1942 these ruthless measures began to take effect. Ten *Gruppen* of Ju 52's, two *Geschwader* and two *Gruppen* of He 111 bombers operating in the transport role, two *Gruppen* of Ju 86's (obsolete bombers used as transports), one *Gruppe* of He 177's, and a composite long range transport *Gruppe* equipped with Fw 200's, Ju 90's and Ju 290's; totalling some 500 aircraft, these units collected in southern Russia. Soon, with the addition of aircraft from the training schools, unit 'hacks', machines snatched from specialist units, this number swelled to nearly 850.

From the very start the Stalingrad supply operations went badly. There was no time for the crews of the newly activated units—many of them straight from training schools in Germany—to accustom themselves to conditions gradually. Instead they were pitch-forked into the operation, to fly in conditions that would daunt the most experienced pilot. The harsh cold of the Russian winter and the atrocious flying weather, the badly equipped airfields, the dangerous approach and return flights over enemy territory in the face of Russian fighters and anti-aircraft fire, the constant bombardment of the airfields within the pocket, all these combined to slow up the airlift. As a result the *Luftwaffe* was able to supply an average of only one hundred tons per day.

In the face of relentless Russian pressure on the ground the Stalingrad pocket shrank steadily, and on January 16th, 1943 the vital airfield at Pitomnik was lost. The secondary airfield at Gumrak was quite inadequate for the needs of the large scale airlift, and the *Luftwaffe* had to resort to air-dropped supplies—a considerably less efficient method. This marked the beginning of the end. Weakened by hunger, the German soldiers were often unable to retrieve canisters which fell in any but the shallowest snow.

When the 91,000 starving survivors at Stalingrad finally surrendered on February 2nd, 1943, the *Luftwaffe* had lost a total of 488 aircraft in its attempt to keep the garrison supplied by air. Of these losses 266 were Ju 52's and 165 were He 111's; most of the crashes were due to take-off and landing accidents at the badly equipped airfields, but towards the end of the airlift Russian fighters became increasingly active.

The serious consequences of the failure at Stalingrad were to run to the very roots of the *Luftwaffe*. The losses in aircraft were serious enough, but these could be replaced with time. Far worse, the aircrew training programme had ground to a halt for want of aircraft and qualified instructors; losses in both had been heavy at Stalingrad, for the Ju 52's from the training schools often lacked even the most rudimentary radio aids to navigation, but they were still sent into the pocket with supplies. Another serious consequence of the airlift was that it caused a serious shortage of aviation fuel; this shortage had first become apparent in the summer of 1942, but instead of the expected lull in operations during the autumn mud season, the fighting had intensified. Now the Germans were forced to make drastic cuts in non-operational flying—and yet again the flying training organisation suffered. The fuel position would be stabilised by the summer of 1943 when more and more of the synthetic oil plants started production, but by then the damage was done. The breakdown in training was to cause great harm to the long term recuperative powers of the *Luftwaffe*.

CHAPTER THREE

The Tide Turns

Gentlemen, we are no longer on the offensive; rather we shall find ourselves for the next one and a half to two years on the defensive. Now these facts are becoming apparent to those in the highest positions of the Luftwaffe, *and are being taken into account in their calculations. Naturally this will mean that we must now have many more fighters, and as many as we possibly can of the (Messerschmitt) 110 and 410 'destroyer' types.*

Generalfeldmarschall Erhard Milch, during a production conference held in Berlin in July 1943.

THE EARLY months of 1943 found the *Luftwaffe* badly over-extended. The defeat at Stalingrad had resulted in serious losses in both aircraft and crews, and now the force was under great pressure not only in Russia, but also in the west and in the Mediterranean. Whereas in the past the Germans had usually been able to take on their opponents one at a time, this was no longer so. No longer could one front be stripped of aircraft while a decisive battle was being fought on another.

The *Luftwaffe* had been designed for the high speed campaigns which had characterised the war's first three years. Then relatively high loss rates were acceptable, provided the end was achieved quickly. And it did not matter too much if aircraft and qualified instructors were syphoned away from the training schools, if the war was going to be over before the student crews would be really needed.

Now, at the beginning of 1943, the position had changed radically. It was now going to be a long war after all, and the *Luftwaffe* was far from prepared for that. Apart from the breakdown of the training programme, there was also a shortage of up-to-date equipment. For the most part the combat types in large scale use were developments of machines in service at the beginning of the war; the sole exception to this was the Focke-Wulf 190 fighter. The two most important replacement types, the Heinkel 177 heavy bomber and the Messerschmitt 210 long range fighter bomber, had run into serious trouble and neither was to go into service in appreciable numbers. As a result Generalfeld-marschall Milch, in charge of production, had to order the German manufacturers to turn out still more of the well proven but ageing Bf 109's, Bf 110's, Ju 87's, Ju 88's and He 111's; the newer versions of the Bf 109 and the Ju 88 were still adequate combat aircraft, but the other three had passed the point where further development would improve them by any appreciable margin.

Not only was it in quality that the Germans were beginning to fall behind their enemies, for there was also a serious shortage of combat aircraft of all types. In an effort to overcome the latter problem Milch had made great strides since he took over his new office at the end of 1941, but there was still a long way to go. Typical of the steps taken to raise production was a programme to increase the labour force by recruiting skilled labour in the occupied countries. To encourage these voluntary workers special inducements—good pay and extra rations—were offered. These were sufficient to attract the outsiders, but not to keep them once the R.A.F. bombing offensive had got under way. Milch discussed the problem with Lucht and Kokotacky from the Messerschmitt Company during one of his production conferences, and the following rather intriguing piece of dialogue resulted:

LUCHT: Recently a new problem has emerged. Of the Frenchmen whom we allowed to go on leave, only half at most have come back.

MILCH: Of the eastern workers eighty per cent don't come back. I wouldn't let them go on leave at all.

KOKOTACKY: We have stopped all leave now.

MILCH: You will have to give them something else to amuse themselves, so that they don't want to go . . .

LUCHT: Once again, it is our top-class specialists that have stayed away.

MILCH: I wouldn't let the top-class specialists out of my hands anyway.

LUCHT: But they are married, and that's what our orders are.

MILCH: Well, they will find something else. You will have to set up a proper brothel there. That's what they are doing everywhere . . . He who works hardest gets a girl. You have only to put your heads together with the Security Service, and tell them to 'fix one for us'. It doesn't matter if it costs something. That is not so bad.

LAHS: There is a special agency that is doing that, called 'Homesteads Ltd'.* They are setting-up those things.

MILCH: Lahs, would you like to see about this for us. I have the impression that you, with your worldly wiseness, know more of these things than I do . . .

LAHS: I only want to say that Oberst Frey does that.

MILCH: That is very intelligent. You can't let the people run round free in the German forests. You have to bring a bit of order into it all.

---

* *Heimstaetten G.m.b.H.*

At the beginning of 1943 the main dispositions of the *Luftwaffe* combat aircraft were as follows:

Eastern front	1,530 aircraft
Western front and home defence	1,445 aircraft
Mediterranean	855 aircraft

That so many were committed in the Mediterranean, previously regarded as an area of only secondary importance, is explained by the newly felt German need to bolster up their Italian ally. The Axis position had deteriorated sharply since the Allied victory at Alamein, followed shortly afterwards by the landings in Algeria and Morocco. As the two Allied armies advanced to meet each other, the German and Italian forces found themselves in the jaws of a vice.

Too late, the much-needed reinforcements in aircraft arrived. By taking the most energetic measures, including the movement of fighter units from the Channel area equipped with the latest version of the Fw 190, the *Luftwaffe* was able to hold its own for a short time in Tunisia, in the face of the numerically superior British Desert Air Force. While the Germans operated from well-prepared bases and had short lines of communications, the British were forced to use hastily cleared strips and were far from their centres of supply.

But for all their efforts the Germans could do no more than delay the inevitable. As the Allied ground forces drew their noose round Bizerta and Tunis tighter and tighter, and the Desert Air Force—re-equipped with the latest marks of the Spitfire—established itself in its new bases, the Axis position got steadily worse. The first to suffer serious casualties were the He 126 and Ju 87 ground attack units, which after a short time had to be withdrawn to Sicily. By April 1943 the whole of the *Luftwaffe* in Africa was in serious difficulties, as the Allied blockade cut off supplies of fuel and spares. Units were thrown together on the small number of airfields remaining and the airfields themselves were pounded by Allied bombers. The final straw came when British and American fighters began to mount standing patrols over the airfields used by the *Luftwaffe*, thus putting an end to effective operations even by the fighters. In the face of constant Allied pressure on the ground the final German defensive line cracked, then broke, and on May 13th, 1943 the German forces remaining in North Africa surrendered. Nearly a quarter of a million men laid down their arms, in a disaster exceeded only by that suffered at Stalingrad.

The loss of North Africa was a serious setback to the Axis cause. But Hitler saw clearly that the decisive battles in 1943 were going to be fought in Russia, and he decreed that the first of these was to be a double pincer movement to cut off the Russian forces in the troublesome salient round Kursk, in the centre of the front. The operation was to bear the code-name 'Citadel'.*

Hitler went to great pains to stress the importance of the operation, which

* *Zitadelle.*

would give the Germans the chance to regain some of the prestige they had lost at Stalingrad. In an order issued on April 15th, 1943, he had stated:

'This attack is of decisive importance. It must succeed quickly and completely. It must put the initiative for this spring and summer in our hands. All preparations must therefore be made with the greatest care and energy; the best units, the best weapons, the best commanders, and large quantities of ammunition shall be committed in the areas of the main effort. Every commander and every man must be filled with the decisive meaning of this attack. The victory of Kursk must have the effect of a beacon for the entire world.'

Accordingly the German army earmarked for the attack, which would be concentrated along a front of only 120 miles, a force of 900,000 men backed by 10,000 guns and 2,700 tanks. In keeping with the importance of the hour Goering concentrated 1,800 combat aircraft in the area to support the twin thrusts. Of these 1,100 belonged to *Luftflotte* 4 under General Otto Dessloch, and were to support the southern arm of the pincer; the remaining 700 aircraft, assigned to Generalmajor Paul Deichmann's *Flieger Division* 1, were to support the one from the north.

But such a build-up on the German side did not pass unnoticed by the Russians, and they began to concentrate their own, numerically superior, forces along the front. Thus the stage was set for the greatest armoured clash of the war. And this time the Russians would not be able to turn to Generals 'Mud' and 'Winter' for help.

The battle of Kursk opened early on the morning of July 5th, 1943, and from the start the *Luftwaffe* units were deeply committed. As in the past, the ground attack and bomber units operated intensively in the battlefield area, in support of the armoured thrusts. The new Hs 129 tank-busting aircraft of the Fourth *Gruppe* of *Schlachtgeschwader* 9, under Hauptmann Bruno Meyer, proved to be particularly effective. On the fourth day of the offensive the unit caught a Russian attack in brigade strength, supported by some forty tanks, out in the open. The four *Staffeln* of the *Gruppe*, each with some sixteen Hs 129's, attacked in relays; as one was in action the other three were moving in to attack or else shuttling back to their base at Miloyanovka, twenty minutes flying time away, to re-arm. The German pilots aimed their 30 mm. tungsten-cored cannon shells at the sides and rear of the tanks, where the armour was thinnest, and knocked out several of them. At the end of the battle, which lasted a little over an hour, the Russian attack had been brought to a halt.

But in spite of the strong air support, the German armoured thrusts on the ground made only slow progress, and suffered serious losses against the strong defensive 'hedgehogs'. Moreover the Russian air force, unsubdued, was often able to penetrate to targets behind the German lines and attack troop concentrations there.

When the claws of the German pincers were firmly stuck in the defences round Kursk, the Russian army launched its counter-offensive. The front line on the central front was in the shape of a reversed letter 'S', with the German salient at Orel in the north pointing eastwards, and the Russian salient at Kursk in the south pointing westwards. On July 11th the Russians launched a series of powerful armoured thrusts against the weakly held Orel salient, and began to gain ground. In a short time the German troops moving on Kursk from the north were thrown on the defensive, and reserves were rushed to the threatened sector. *Luftflotte* 6 went into action round Orel, in the hope of stopping or at least slowing the Russians so as to give the German troops time to consolidate their position. At first the Russian advance was through close wooded country-side, and the aircraft could do little to hinder them. Then the armoured force emerged into the open and, with virtually no German ground troops to stop it, began to advance rapidly westwards. The only hope was the *Luftwaffe* anti-tank and ground attack aircraft, and these now rose to the challenge. In a day-long battle, relays of these machines bombed and straffed the Russians, with the result that the attacking force was once again slowed down sufficiently long for the German troops to prepare defensive positions.

But such a pace of operations was maintained only at a high cost in trained men, aircraft and fuel, and the ground attack units began to run short of all three. Of these the recurring famine in fuel was the most serious, and as a result many requests for air support had to be refused.

For the Russians, operating along relatively short lines of communication, there was no similar hindrance. By keeping up a strong pressure on the Orel salient they were able to force the Germans out of it altogether. Further Russian counter-attacks at the south of Kursk forced the Germans back past their start line there as well; by July 23rd, less than three weeks after the opening of the Kursk offensive, it was clear that it had failed disastrously. It was to be the last full scale German offensive to be launched in the east.

Even before the Kursk battle had come to an end, the Germans were forced to turn their attention to the Mediterranean. On July 3rd, 1943 the strength of the *Luftwaffe* in this area was as follows:

	Central Med.	Eastern Med.	Total
Long range bombers	260	40	300
Dive bombers	—	65	65
Single engined fighters	380	70	450
Twin engined fighters	100	10	110
Ground attack	150	—	150
Reconnaissance	85	70	155
Coastal	—	50	50
Total	975	305	1,280

On that day the Allies began large scale air attacks on the German airfields in preparation for the assault on Sicily; by the time the troops landed, one week later, the Germans had lost more than a hundred aircraft. Many of the Sicilian airfields had been made unserviceable, and all the surviving Fw 190 fighter-bombers were withdrawn to the Naples area. As a result the German air effort was almost entirely defensive, and in the face of overwhelming Allied air superiority the bomber force was able to do little. The incessant air attacks rendered the remaining airfields in Sicily useless even as advanced landing grounds. Operating from airfields in the toe of Italy a force of about 100 fighters and fighter-bombers endeavoured to provide some sort of air cover during the final phase of the German withdrawal from Sicily, but they suffered heavily in the process.

While all this had been happening, the R.A.F. night bombing offensive had begun to take on a more menacing note. Since the beginning of 1943 the bombers, led by Pathfinder aircraft fitted with the advanced *H2S* and *Oboe* radar devices, had proved able to find and hit targets even on the darkest of nights. Amongst others, Essen, Dusseldorf, Krefeld and Wuppertal had suffered severe damage as a result. At the same time General Kammhuber's force of radar-controlled night fighters had also increased, and by the end of June 1943 it stood at 554 aircraft.

But while the effectiveness of the night fighter defences had steadily risen, that of the *Flak* arm began to fall away as more and more of its specialised and able-bodied members were transferred to the Eastern Front, and their places were taken by old men, boys, and turncoat Russian prisoners. One of the newcomers recalls:

'On the 15th January 1943, a week before my 16th birthday, my class of 15 and 16 year old boys was called up for duty with the *Flak*. Our battery was a heavy one with four, later six, 10.5 cm guns, in an emplacement at Spandau-Johannisstift on the western suburbs of Berlin. The battery establishment consisted of two officers, thirty N.C.O.'s and other ranks, about a hundred of us boys, and roughly thirty Russian prisoners. The prisoners and the soldiers did the heavier manual jobs. The boys carried out nearly all the tasks, from radio operator to gunner—even the K3 (gun loader). You can imagine that it was hard work for a 15 year old boy to load a gun with 10.5 cm ammunition during rapid fire (each shell weighed 32 lbs) often with the barrel pointing upwards at an angle of 40 degrees or more. The most skilful job was that of range-finder, often a boy too. Sometimes the commander would allow one of us to give the fire commands, the most exalted position of all: "*Achtung! ... Gruppe! ... Achtung! Gruppe!* (Attention! ... Salvo!)" If the battle was only a short one the fire discipline was usually very good. But woe if the battery fired more than eighty or one hundred rounds! Each gun crew had the ambition to be the best and to fire the most ammunition. Instead of a fine unison crash there would be guns firing off all over the place. We boys were most enthusiastic, and it was a bad day when there was no British activity. Our feelings were not completely selfless, since after a raid we were allowed to sleep-in in the morning, and did not have to go to school.'

The fighter and *Flak* defences combined to take a serious toll of the night raiders, and during the month of June 1943 they shot down 275 of them.

Then, on July 25th, the R.A.F. introduced its own answer to the German defences: *Window. Window* was the code name given to the bundles of strips of metal foil, each one cut to one half the wavelength of the German precision radar sets. Dropped at a rate of one per minute from each aircraft in the attacking force, the bundles broke up to form clouds of radar-reflective strips; the 'clouds' combined to form a 'smokescreen' through which radar controlled fighter interceptions and gun engagements were impossible. The new tactics were first used during a 791 bomber attack on Hamburg, and reduced the entire German defensive system to utter chaos; as a result only 12 aircraft, 1.5 per cent of the force, were lost. In equally successful follow-up attacks on July 28th and 29th, and August 2nd, large sections of the city of Hamburg were burned to the ground and 50,000 people were killed.

Following the fiasco over Hamburg, the German night fighters tactics underwent a sweeping reorganisation. The *Himmelbett* method of close ground control gave way to two new tactical methods, *Wild Boar* and *Tame Boar.** The *Wild Boar* tactics called for the concentration of night fighter units over the target itself, where the massed searchlights and the Pathfinders' marker flares lit up the sky for miles around, to silhouette the bombers for the fighters. Thus the latter could now attack without using radar; this was significant, because it meant that *Window* radar jamming had no effect upon the system. Major Hajo Herrmann set up a *Geschwader* of single-seat Bf 109's and Fw 190's, to exploit the new tactics.

The two-seater radar equipped specialist night fighters could also engage in *Wild Boar*-type tactics over the target. But to use their potential to the full Oberst Victor von Lossberg, a night fighter expert, devised the *Tame Boar* method. Under this system the now-jammed ground radar stations were to direct the fighters to where the *Window* concentration was densest, and once they were there the German pilots were to search for the bombers visually.

During the late summer of 1943 the *Luftwaffe* night fighter force began to adjust itself to its new tactics. But it took time, and in the interim the R.A.F. was able to cause serious damage.

While *Window* gave the R.A.F. night bomber crews a measure of relief from the attentions of the German defences, there was no such respite for their American colleagues who attacked in daylight. During the early part of 1943

* *Wilde Sau* and *Zahme Sau.*

the U.S.A.A.F. attacks on targets in Germany had been few and far between, experimental in character, and modest in scale. But by July these had increased in effectiveness to a point where they could no longer be treated lightly. The *Luftwaffe* was forced to pull back more and more fighters from the periphery of Hitler's uneasy empire, in order to protect the homeland. By August 1943 the force thus committed and ready for operations comprised some 400 single engined fighters, Bf 109's and Fw 190's, and some 80 twin engined fighters, Bf 110's and Me 410's. The twin engined types, known to the Germans as 'Destroyers',* were especially potent against the American bombers; they had the range to enable them to fight long running battles with the attacking formations, and moreover they carried a heavier armament than the single engined types.

This, then, was the position on the morning of August 17th, 1943, when a force of 146 Fortresses, escorted by Spitfires and Thunderbolts, crossed the Dutch coast bound for the Messerschmitt works at Regensburg. Though fully alerted, the defenders did not go into action immediately. Instead they waited until the formation neared the German border, when the short range escort fighters were forced by lack of fuel to turn round and go home. Then the *Luftwaffe* pounced. In a series of concentrated attacks, relays of fighter *Gruppen* tore into the bomber formations, and the subsequent running battle continued up to and past the target, for a distance of some 350 miles. When the depleted American force arrived in North Africa after crossing the length of occupied Europe, it was short by 24 bombers.

But the day's battle was not yet over. Even before the first wave of bombers had reached Regensburg a second wave, comprising 229 Fortresses, was making for the vitally important ball-bearing works at Schweinfurt. This time the Germans did not even wait for the fighter escort to withdraw before going in to attack. While single engined fighters held off the Thunderbolt escort, others swept in to rake the Fortresses with cannon and machine gun fire. When the escorts finally did turn for home single and twin engined *Gruppen* arrived, and launched salvoes of 210 mm rocket bombs, each with a warhead weighing 90 pounds, into the dense bomber formations from outside the range of the defending .5 inch machine guns. Thirty-six bombers failed to return from the Schweinfurt attack.

The twin attacks on Regensburg and Schweinfurt cost the Americans sixty Fortresses—sixteen per cent of the force engaged—and a further one hundred bombers had been damaged, many of them beyond repair. This reverse led to a revision of the American bombing policy, and from then until October 7th only three out of the fifteen heavy bomber raids were against targets in Germany —and none of these were penetrations in depth.

After the capture of Sicily there could be little doubt that the Western
* *Zerstoerer.*

Allies' next move would be the invasion of Italy itself. But because of the needs of the home front the heavy losses suffered by the *Luftwaffe* in Sicily could not be made good. When the Allies did land on the toe of Italy, on September 3rd, the German strength in the Mediterranean was down to a total of 880 aircraft. As a result Generalfeldmarschall von Richthofen decided to hold back his force for the decisive battles that would certainly follow, and the initial German reaction was weak.

On September 9th the Italians capitulated, and on that morning the Italian battle fleet set sail from La Spezia for Malta, to surrender. The Third *Gruppe* of K.G. 100 had been standing by at Istres for just such an eventuality, and the *Geschwader* commander, Major Bernhard Jope, led his bombers into action. For the first time in a large scale attack, III./K.G. 100 were to make use of the Fritz X guided bomb; this weapon comprised a normal 3,300 pound armour piercing bomb, with a radio control mechanism built into the tail to enable the missile to be controlled during the final part of its trajectory. Jope's men caught the Italian fleet as it neared the narrow straits that separate Corsica and Sardinia, and scored two direct hits on the battleship *Roma*. The resultant fire reached the ship's magazine and she blew up, broke into two, and sank. Shortly afterwards her sister ship, the *Italia*, was also hit; she took on 800 tons of water, but was able to reach Malta under her own steam.

On the same day as the Italian fleet sailed, Allied troops landed at Salerno near Naples. Here was a large concentration of shipping, just the sort of target for which the Fritz X had been designed. Jope's men pressed home their attacks, and in the next ten days they scored hits on the battleship H.M.S. *Warspite*, and the cruisers H.M.S. *Uganda* and U.S.S. *Savannah*, causing serious damage to all three. Other units attacked the ships with Henschel 293 glider bombs, but at Salerno these weapons achieved little. Meanwhile German fighter-bombers, including Bf 109's equipped with 210 mm rocket launchers for use against ground targets, maintained a steady pressure against the troops ashore. The *Luftwaffe* effort kept up until September 20th, when British troops advancing from the toe of Italy began to threaten their airfields in the Foggia area and the shorter range units were forced to pull back beyond range.

The lull in the American long-penetration attacks lasted until October 8th, 1943, when during a week of intensive action Bremen, Marienburg, Danzig and Muenster were all hit. These attacks met the full vigour of the German defences, and cost the Americans 83 bombers. But the climax came on October 14th, when 291 Fortresses again made for Schweinfurt. This time the German reaction was, in the words of the American historians, 'unprecedented in its magnitude, in the cleverness with which it was planned, and in the severity with which it was executed'. Again wave upon wave of cannon-armed fighters made concentrated attacks on the bomber formations at close range, while others launched their rockets and fired heavy calibre cannon from outside the range of the defensive fire. Once bombers had been damaged and were unable to keep up with the formation, they were shot down almost at leisure. Many of the single engined fighters were able to refuel and re-arm after their first attack, and go into action again as the bombers made their homeward flights. The result was a crippling disaster for the American Eighth Air Force. Sixty Fortresses were shot down, seventeen had suffered severe damage, and a further 121 had been damaged less heavily. Thus of the original force of 291 heavy bombers which had set out, 198 were either destroyed or damaged. In return the Fortresses had been able to shoot down only 38 of the German fighters, and cause damage to 20 more.

So it was that the Americans learnt that even their incompatibly heavily armed and armoured bombers could not afford to trade blow for blow with the defending fighters. But as is the way with that vigorous people, they refused to admit defeat and instead went forward to prove that the lessons of the Battle of Britain were not absolute, and that daylight bombing in the face of powerful defences could be made a paying proposition. When they did, the *Luftwaffe* was to suffer the greatest of its many disasters.

CHAPTER FOUR

The Losing Battle

War is the shock of two opposing forces in collision with each other, from which it follows as a matter of course that the stronger not only destroys the other, but carries it forward with it in its movement.
Generalmajor Carl von Clausewitz, On War, *published in 1832.*

The enemy knows that he must wipe out our fighters. Once he has done that he will be able to play football with the German people.
Generalfeldmarschall Erhard Milch, *during a conference held in Berlin in March 1944.*

For a short time at the beginning of 1944, the *Luftwaffe* High Command had some grounds for thinking that the worst might be over. The day fighters had fought the American daylight attacks to a standstill, while the night fighter force's new tactics had largely overcome the *Window* menace. The eastern front had been stabilised after a hard year's fighting, and in Italy the Allies were making only the slowest progress.

Thanks to Milch's vigorous efforts in stepping up the production of aircraft the equipment position had improved greatly during 1943, as may be seen from the following table:

	First Line Strength	
	January 1st, 1943	January 1st, 1944
Long range bombers	1,135	1,580
Ground attack aircraft	270	610
Single engined fighters	1,245	1,535
Twin engined fighters	495	905
Reconnaissance aircraft	675	755
Coastal types	135	200
	3,955	5,585

Moreover, new types were at last becoming available. Ground attack versions of the Fw 190 fighter were being produced in useful numbers to replace the out-dated Ju 87; Ju 188 and He 177 bombers had begun to replace some of the

Ju 88's and He 111's; Me 410 and He 219 fighters had started replacing the ageing Bf 110 in the heavy fighter and night fighter units respectively. For the future the white hope was the advanced Me 262 jet fighter, due to be in large scale service by the summer, to be followed by the equally promising Arado 234 jet bomber shortly afterwards; the prototypes of both these machines were already flying.

On the strategic bombardment side two spectacular new weapons were beginning to roll off the production lines, the Fiesler 103 flying bomb and the A-4 long range rocket.* With such weapons in large scale use, the former cheap enough to be launched in such numbers as to swamp the defences, the latter unstoppable once it had been launched, it seemed that the Germans would be able to flatten London and smash any attempt to assemble a force for the invasion of France.

There were other grounds for satisfaction. The fuel situation had improved markedly since the summer of 1943, and the slackening off in operations at the end of the year had combined with record production to produce fuel reserves greater than at any time since 1941. Moreover the training of new aircrews had improved greatly since the hiatus at the time of Stalingrad, though there was still room for much improvement in this field.†

But for the Germans the feeling of euphoria was in fact just the lull before the storm, and the first month of the new year brought them back to ugly reality. They had not seen the end of the daylight battles, merely the end of the beginning. The American answer to the German fighter defences was basically the same as that tried by the *Luftwaffe* during the Battle of Britain, namely the escort fighter. By fitting the Thunderbolts and Mustangs with droppable fuel tanks, these single seater machines were able to accompany the bomber formations deep into German territory. But the American long range fighters were far from being lame ducks compared with the defending fighters, as the Bf 110 had been over Britain. Indeed, the Mustang with its thin laminar-flow wing was able to outperform all-comers. The drop tanks shaved 35 m.p.h. off its top speed; once these had been released it was more than 50 m.p.h. faster than the Bf 109's and Fw 190's then in service, and could turn tighter and dive faster than either of the German types.

On January 4th, 1944 Mustangs accompanied bombers to Kiel and Muenster, and the next day Thunderbolts went as far south as Bordeaux. By March Mustangs were flying with two larger 75 gallon drop tanks and had a radius of

* These are commonly known in Britain as the V1 and the V2 respectively; the 'V' stood for the German word *Vergeltungswaffe*, meaning 'reprisal weapon'. The A-4 rocket was controlled not by the *Luftwaffe* but by the German army, and therefore comes outside the compass of this volume.

† At this time German fighter pilots received approximately 160 flying hours in training before going into action; British pilots received 360 hours, American pilots more than 400.

action of 650 miles—as far as Berlin; a little later two 108 gallon drop tanks were carried, and the radius of action went up to 850 miles—sufficient to cover any likely target within Germany or occupied Europe.

Under the command of the energetic Major General William Kepner, the aggressive American escort fighters went from strength to strength. Kepner did not fall into the trap of tying his pilots to the immediate vicinity of the bombers, but instead allowed junior commanders on the spot to exercise their own judgement on whether or not to pursue the enemy. During the long approach flights the escorting fighters were forced to weave or orbit to stay with the bombers, and this drastically reduced their effective radius of action. The Americans turned this problem to their advantage by furnishing relays of fighters to take over the escort at intervals of about 200 miles along the route. Once relieved of their responsibility to the bombers, the returning fighters were told to fan out and use their remaining ammunition on targets of opportunity both in the air and on the ground. Now no aircraft with crosses on could consider itself safe anywhere during the day: unarmed courier, transport or training aircraft going about their business, even new aircraft under test, all were liable to be pounced on by the returning escorts.

The result of all this was a disaster for the *Luftwaffe*. Amongst the first to suffer heavily were the German twin engined 'Destroyer' units. On March 16th, for example, forty-three Bf 110's of the Third *Gruppe* of *Zerstoerergeschwader 76* ran in to attack a formation of Fortresses near Augsburg. While they were thus engaged the powerful Mustang escort struck. In the one-sided battle that followed the Messerschmitts were hounded all the way back to base, and twenty-six were shot down. Within a short time the twin engined day fighter units were forced to cease operations against the American bombers altogether.

Prior to the arrival of the long range escorts the tendency had been to increase the hitting power of the German single engined fighters, so that they could knock down the tough American bombers more easily. But the extra armament meant extra weight, which in turn placed the interceptor pilots in an even worse position if they had to dog-fight with the escorts. In an effort to overcome this problem Generalmajor Adolf Galland, the German fighter commander, set up separate 'heavy' and 'light' fighter *Gruppen*. The former were equipped with heavily armed and armoured versions of the Fw 190 and the Bf 109 and were to go for the bombers, while the latter were to fend off the escorts and used lightly armed Bf 109's with specially uprated engines. But these tactics did not produce a lasting answer: the American escort fighters were often present in such overwhelming numbers that they were able to overcome the German escort and get in amongst the 'heavy' fighters, where they did great execution. In April Generalmajor Galland reported to his superiors:

'Between January and April 1944 our day fighter arm lost more than one thousand pilots. They included our best *Staffel, Gruppe* and *Geschwader* commanders. Each incursion of the enemy is costing us about fifty aircrew. The time has come when our force is within sight of collapse.'

The less well-trained replacement pilots proved no match for their American foes, who grew more confident and aggressive with each month that passed. The Germans were beginning to lose control of the airspace over their own country.

However, the means of salvation for the Germans lay close at hand: the new Me 262 jet fighter. The great significance of this aircraft was that with its top speed of 540 m.p.h. it was fast enough to avoid even the Mustangs, while at the same time its immensely powerful battery of four 30 mm. cannon was easily able to tear the American bombers to pieces.

Ironically, the undoing of the Me 262 as far as the German pilots were concerned was that it was *too* good: the machine could also be modified to carry two 550 pound bombs. Hitler immediately saw in this a means of wiping out any Allied seaborne invasion attempt—and there can be little doubt that had sufficient of these fighter-bombers been available, they could have seriously embarrassed the planned invasion of France. Accordingly at the end of 1943 he said that the Me 262 should be used initially as a fighter-bomber. The counter-arguments of Goering, Milch and the leading fighter commanders served only to strengthen his resolve, and did so to such a degree that early in 1944 he ordered that *none* of the Me 262's should be built as fighters alone. Generalfeldmarschall Milch later recalled: *

'Hitler believed that the fighter pilots were living a good life, in their messes, and only now and again would they fly off to do rather gentlemanly battle with the enemy. Meanwhile the men on the ground were suffering great hardships and were getting no help. First he had done too much for the fighters; then later he was for the bombers, because he believed that only they would help the army.'

One can perhaps understand Hitler's great sympathy for the foot soldier wallowing in the mud at the front—he had, after all, been one of them during the First World War. Nevertheless his decision regarding the Me 262 was a mistake of the greatest magnitude; the jet fighter had to be re-stressed for the bomber role, and this resulted in a delay of about six months in the large scale production of the type. The outcome was that instead of being available in useful numbers as a fighter in March 1944, when it could have inflicted losses on the Schweinfurt scale on the American heavy bombers, it did not become operational as a bomber until September 1944, when the moment of decision had passed and it could achieve little.

In the late summer of 1943 the R.A.F. *Window* jamming had reduced the German night fighter force to near chaos. The new visual interception *Wild*

* During a conversation with the author.

Boar and *Tame Boar* tactics had, in the absence of any new radar equipment able to see through the *Window* 'smokescreen', been introduced as a stop-gap to provide the German cities with at least some form of defence against the crushing British night bombing attacks. Meanwhile, the attackers had constantly introduced new tactics and equipment, in an effort to retain the initiative.

Both of the German night fighting methods were dependent upon the aircrews receiving accurate and up-to-date information on the position of the British bomber streams. But if the German aircrews could be prevented from receiving this information then the whole system could be set to nought. It was with this in mind that the R.A.F. had stepped up its jamming of the German radio control channels in the autumn of 1943.

In response to this new jamming offensive the Germans multiplied the number of radio channels used to communicate with their fighters, and in this way they diluted the British jamming effort. Meanwhile, the German aircrews were becoming more proficient in their new tactics and this, coupled with the introduction of the SN-2 night fighter radar set which was able to see through the 'smokescreen' of *Window*, enabled them to take an increasingly heavy toll of the attackers.

On January 21st, 1944, 55 bombers were shot down out of 648 attacking Magdeburg, and a week later 43 out of 683 attacking Berlin. Even these great scores were eclipsed on February 19th, when 78 out of a force of 823 attacking Leipzig were shot down. The hard-fought battle between Bomber Command and the German night defences was now nearing its climax. Between the large battles were many smaller ones, and the war diary of *Nachtjagdgeschwader* 6 for a twelve-day period during March 1944 gives some idea of the intensity of the actions then being fought, as seen through German eyes. N.J.G. 6 operated as part of the Seventh Fighter Division, responsible for the defence of southern Germany. The *Geschwader* was not at full strength, comprising only two *Gruppen* of Bf 110's, the First at Mainz/Finthen and the Second at Stuttgart/Echterdingen. The unit also operated a few Ju 88's to seek out and report on the position of the bomber streams, and drop flares to mark them.

March 15th. Target Stuttgart. Own take-off was too early, and as a result fuel began to run low. Twenty-six Bf 110's and three Ju 88's took off. Three four-engined bombers shot down for certain, and two probables. Five Bf 110's crashed because they ran out of fuel, one more made a belly landing, and one force-landed at Zürich/Duebendorf (in Switzerland). (R.A.F. losses that night, 36 out of 863.)

March 18th. British penetration into the area Frankfurt-Mannheim-Darmstadt (the target was Frankfurt). Twenty-four Bf 110's and two Ju 88's took off. One bomber was shot down for certain, and there were three probables. One Bf 110 was shot down, and one was rammed by an enemy night fighter and crashed. (R.A.F. losses, 22 out of 846.)

March 22nd. Target Frankfurt. Twenty-one Bf 110's and two Ju 88's set out. Oberleutnant Becker* scored six victories. The air situation was not at all clear. The enemy turned when to the north of Terschelling, towards the south-east in the direction of Osnabrueck, but this was not recognised. It was from Osnabrueck on that contact was made. The enemy main force was not recognised until it was just to the north of Frankfurt. (R.A.F. losses, 33 out of 816.)

March 23rd. Received false reports of an enemy force moving in an easterly direction. The target was Paris (in fact it was Laon). Twenty Bf 110's and one Ju 88 took off, but in vain. (R.A.F. losses, 2 out of 143.)

March 24th. The enemy approached over the North Sea and Jutland, to Berlin. The return flight touched the northern tip of our own divisional area. Radio Beacon 12 was subjected to interference. Crews encountered severe icing when breaking through the overcast. Vain attempts were made to make contact with the bomber stream during its return flight. Our own flares over Berlin were too high (20,000 feet). Very disciplined firing by the *Flak* over Berlin.† Corps communication channels could be heard well, in spite of the enemy interference. In action were eleven Bf 110's to Berlin, five Bf 110's against the returning stream, 3 Bf 110's engaged in *Himmelbett* operations, and one Ju 88 reconnaissance aircraft. One victory to Oberleutnant Becker. (R.A.F. losses, 72 out of 811—obviously other *Geschwader* did better.)

March 26th. About 500 bombers approached over the Zuider Zee on an easterly course towards the Rhine. They then turned south towards Essen-Oberhausen-Duisburg (the target was Essen). Our radar and ground observers recognised the turn too late. Our own reconnaissance aircraft, a Ju 88 flown by Hauptmann Wallner, reported enemy activity over the Ruhr area as a whole. The direction of the (enemy's) approach and return flights could not be recognised from the running commentary. Therefore it was not possible to get into the bomber stream. Due to the devious approach and the strong headwind, II./N.J.G. 6 did not arrive at the target before the attack had ended. Severe icing was reported. Twenty-one Bf 110's on *Tame Boar* operations, three Bf 110's on *Himmelbett*, one Ju 88 on reconnaissance. Three Bf 110's ran out of fuel and crashed, and one made a belly landing. (R.A.F. losses, 9 out of 705.)

The German pilots were ordered to pursue the raiders to the limit of their endurance, and once contact had been made they were to break off the action only when their fuel had almost run out. There was thus little reserve in hand if the fighter became lost while, say, chasing a corkscrewing bomber. So losses due to fighters running out of fuel were risked and accepted—this was all part and parcel of the *Tame Boar* tactics. The German aircrewmen were quite

---

* Martin Becker was to end the war as a Hauptmann, with 57 victories.
† That is to say the gunners held their fire, while the night fighters engaged.

prepared to take the risks.   This was their own equivalent of the Battle of Britain, and they fought to defend their homes and loved ones with the same ferocity that their British counterparts had in 1940.

And the combination of familiar and efficient tactics, the acceptance of risks, and the new SN-2 radar device, was paying off.

The climax of the night bombing offensive came on the night of March 30th. 1944, when 781 Lancasters and Halifaxes set out to bomb Nuremburg.   It was a moonlight night and very cold, so that the bombers streamed dense white condensation trails behind them.   Moreover, the strong winds at high altitude caused the bomber stream to lose its cohesion, and the aircraft scattered over a wide area.   On this occasion the German control and reporting organisation worked perfectly, and twenty-one *Gruppen* of night fighters—about 200 aircraft—went into action.   The result was a disaster for R.A.F. Bomber Command: 94 bombers were shot down, and a further 46 were damaged.

Just as Schweinfurt marked a turning point in the fortunes of the American bombers, so Nuremburg was one for the British.   The reasons for this we shall see later.   Meanwhile Bomber Command now shifted its main effort to communications targets in less well-defended France and Belgium, in preparation for the forthcoming invasion.   For the first time since the summer of 1940 the German cities enjoyed a respite at night.

While the German defences battled, with varying fortunes, against the British and American bomber fleets, the Germans' own attempts at strategic attacks on Britain met with little success.   The bomber attack on Britain, code-named Operation Ibex* by the *Luftwaffe*, opened on January 21st, 1944 with an attack on London, and finally petered out at the end of May.   It caused little damage to the capital or the other cities attacked, and the bomber units involved suffered heavy losses.

The launching sites for the Fi 103 flying bombs, being erected along the north coast of France had been detected early on by R.A.F. reconnaissance aircraft; their significance was soon realised, and before they became operational they were 'taken out' by striking forces of light and medium bombers of the Allied tactical air forces.   Moreover, the delivery of completed flying bombs was so erratic that the opening of this 'robot bombardment' had to be put back again and again.

On June 6th, 1944 the Western Allies launched their long-awaited invasion of France.   To oppose the landings Generalfeldmarschall Sperrle, commanding *Luftflotte* 3 in France and Belgium, could muster a mere 198 bombers and 125 fighters;   in addition *Fliegerkorps* X in the south had some 200 anti-shipping aircraft, many of them equipped to launch Fritz X and Hs 293 missiles.   Against these the Allies put up more than three thousand bombers and five thousand

* *Unternehmen Steinbock.*

fighters. The result was that German units attempting to penetrate to the Normandy area by day were cut to pieces. The anti-shipping units attempted to attack by night, but even then they suffered losses out of all proportion to the meagre results they achieved; during the first ten days of the invasion only five ships were lost to direct air attack.

In the end the Germans abandoned the idea of direct attacks on the ships, and instead devoted their efforts to mining the narrow seas. In the following six weeks more than three thousand mines of various types were sown, including many of the new pressure mines which could be countered only by restricting all movement to a snail's pace while in shallow water. By the end of July the mining campaign had caused the loss of seven destroyers, two minesweepers, and seventeen merchantmen and auxiliary vessels. The mines caused considerable inconvenience, but such losses were not going to turn away the greatest invasion armada ever assembled.

The safe arrival of the invasion force in France released the Allied strategic bombing forces from the 'softening up' task, and now these were able to concentrate on the Achilles' heel of the German war economy: oil. In short order the synthetic oil plants that dotted Germany, at Bruex, Boehlen and Leuna, Luetzendorf, Zwickau and Magdeburg, Ruhland, Zeitz and Poelitz, all suffered heavily. By routeing in its bombers over France where the German air reporting organisation was now virtually non-existent, the R.A.F. was able to avoid the worst attentions of the German defences; furthermore, the night bombers now had their own fighter and radar jamming support, from the newly operational No. 100 Group.

The effect of these day and night attacks on the refineries was immediate and devastating. Production of aviation fuel fell from 195,000 tons in May to 52,000 tons in June. The attacks continued, and things went from bad to worse. In July only 35,000 tons were produced, in August 16,000 tons and in September a paltry 7,000 tons. With consumption running at 150,000 tons during the month of July, even the reserve of half a million tons accumulated during the winter could not stave off the inevitable.

The first to suffer, as always, were the flying training schools, many of which had to be shut down; their partially trained pilots were sent to serve in the infantry. Next came the bomber units, many of which were disbanded. Reconnaissance flights were severely limited, fighter-bomber support was permitted only in 'decisive situations', and only fighter operations in air defence were allowed to continue without restriction. The only aircraft not affected by the critical fuel shortage were the jets, which ran on low grade fuel which was available in relative abundance.

On the night of June 12th, 1944, six months later than had originally been planned, the first Fi 103 flying bomb hit London. The plan for the first night of the bombardment had called for two large salvoes of missiles aimed at London, one at 11 p.m. and the other at 4 a.m. the next morning; in the event so many sites reported themselves unserviceable that only ten bombs were launched—four reached England, one of which impacted on the capital. After this wobbly start there was a delay of three days before firing was resumed, to continue until the end of the month with between 120 and 190 bombs per day.

Oberst Wachtel's *Flak* Regiment 155 (W), responsible for launching the flying bombs, kept up this rate of firing throughout July and most of August, though the rate began to tail off towards the end as one after another of the launching sites were captured by Allied ground forces. At 4 a.m. on the morning of September 1st the initial phase of the attack came to an end, after 8,564 flying bombs had been launched at London.

With the capture of the ground launching sites the *Luftwaffe* began to employ He 111's as airborne launchers for the flying bombs. Soon an entire *Geschwader*, K.G. 53, with over a hundred Heinkels, was engaged on this work. The single flying bomb tucked under the wing between the port engine and the fuselage imposed a severe performance penalty on the already outmoded bombers, and to survive in the face of the overwhelming British defences the German crews had to operate at night and at low level. The carrier aircraft would make their approach flights low down over the sea at 300 feet, below the cover of the British radar chain, and make a brief 'pop up' to 1,500 feet when some forty miles from the target to launch their missiles. Then the German crews would return to low level to return home.

The intermittent stand-off bombing attacks continued into 1945, and ended when the final air-launched flying bomb crashed near Hornsey on the morning of January 14th. Of a total of about 1,200 missiles launched from the air, only 638 crossed the coast of England or were otherwise seen by the defences. Of these only one in ten reached its target, the remainder failing either because of the missile's inherent inaccuracy or else because they were cut down by the defences.

The autumn of 1944 had seen the near-eclipse of the *Luftwaffe* bomber, reconnaissance and ground attack units. On all fronts the force could maintain only a desultory pace of operations. As one German soldier in the west put it: 'If the aircraft were camouflaged, we knew that they were British; if they were silver, we knew that they were American; and if they weren't there at all, we knew that they were German!' But in the autumn the German synthetic oil industry was able to recover in part from the pounding it had suffered in the summer, and as plants were gradually brought back into production the output of aviation fuel rose; in October 18,000 tons were produced, in November 39,000 tons. Used astutely this was to be sufficient to inject, temporarily, a new life into the almost paralysed *Luftwaffe*

A further factor which played its part at this time was the delivery of more and more of the jet types—Me 262's and Ar 234's—to the front line units. By September Hitler had relented a little on the question of the use of the Me 262 as a fighter; after the Fuehrer Conference held between the 21st and the 23rd of that month the diary of Karl-Otto Saur, the official in charge of fighter production, recorded that Hitler had agreed that:

'The Ar 234 will, with all possible despatch, continue to be turned out as a bomber in the greatest possible numbers. As it is possible to use this aircraft for the short range targets with three 1,100 pound bombs, and for long range targets with one 1,100 pound bomb, under considerably more favourable general conditions than the (Me) 262 when used as a bomber, the Fuehrer confirms his earlier promise that, for every single battleworthy 234 accepted as a bomber, the General in charge of fighters will be allocated one battleworthy 262 fighter.'

The lull in the fighting during the late autumn of 1944 served the Germans well, and under conditions of the greatest secrecy the *Luftwaffe* assembled an impressively strong force of combat aircraft along the western front. This comprised the following:

Long range bombers	55
Jet bombers	40
Ground attack aircraft	390
Single engined fighters	1,770
Twin engined fighters	140
Reconnaissance aircraft	65
	2,460

More important than the number of aircraft was the fact that the Germans had husbanded sufficient fuel to enable the force to go into action. This was to be the air cover for Hitler's last desperate gamble in the west: Operation 'Watch on the Rhine'.* A force of two hundred thousand men, including seven *Panzer* divisions, was to punch a path through the weakly held Ardennes sector of the Anglo-American front, and attempt to take the vitally important supply port of Antwerp, more than eighty miles away.

The *Luftwaffe* task during the offensive was to be a twofold one. First, it was to eliminate the opposing air force by means of an all-out surprise attack on their forward airfields, after which an umbrella of fighters was to seal off the battle zone. Second, with air superiority thus secured, the ground attack units were to provide close support for the fighting troops, while bomber and night ground attack aircraft were to strike at enemy reserves and reinforcements. So much for the plan.

* *Unternehmen Wacht am Rhein.*

The German offensive opened on the morning of December 16th, 1944, but without the planned knock-out blow against the Allied airfields: thick fog during this and for most of the following eight days seriously hampered air operations by both sides. But the Germans had far more to gain than to lose by such a state of affairs, and initially the ground forces made substantial gains. On December 17th the cloud base lifted a little and German close support aircraft flew some 600 sorties, for the most part ground strafing missions; that night bombers and fighters flew nearly 300 more sorties against Allied troops moving up. But gradually Allied resistance stiffened, as combat units were moved in from other parts of France and Belgium to stem the advance. By December 20th the spearheads of the German attack, which had in places advanced nearly fifty miles from their start positions, had been forced to halt.

On December 24th the fog finally lifted, and now the *Luftwaffe* felt the full weight of the Allied aerial strength; on that day eleven of its more important airfields were severely damaged, and numerous others suffered less so. When the newer German pilots did attempt to do battle with Allied fighters the disparity between the training they had received and that of their older comrades soon became evident; as one R.A.F. pilot put it: 'The good German pilots were very good indeed; the rest were pathetic'. Thus the *Luftwaffe* suffered heavily in its stand-up fight with the Allied air forces. Meanwhile on Christmas Day the re-grouped American ground forces had taken the offensive, and the German troops were being forced back to their start lines.

Then, on New Year's Day 1945, the *Luftwaffe* launched its belated attempt at a knock-out blow against the Allied forward airfields: Operation Ground Plate.* The force of more than 800 piston engined fighters, with a sprinkling of jet types, was directed against seventeen Allied airfields in France, Holland and Belgium. At the head of each single seat fighter *Gruppe* flew two Ju 88 night fighters acting as pilot aircraft, to guide the less experienced pilots to their targets.

The blow achieved complete surprise; it cost the Allies 134 aircraft destroyed, and a further 62 damaged beyond unit repair. But the attack of ground targets in a high performance aircraft is an exacting task, especially if the targets are heavily defended by anti-aircraft fire. It proved to be beyond the ability of many of the new German pilots. There was great confusion at some of the targets; aircraft got in each other's way, and there were some collisions. The net result was that the *Luftwaffe* lost about 200 aircraft and their pilots.

So it was that the *Luftwaffe* units equipped with piston engined aircraft went out in a final blaze of glory. For the rest of the war they were able to take little part in the proceedings. Not that the operations were limited by any shortage of aircraft, or even the men to fly them. But the renewal of the Anglo-American strategic bombing offensive against the synthetic oil producing

* *Unternehmen Bodenplatte.*

plants, in December, strangled supplies of high grade aviation fuel, and the Ardennes offensive had bitten deeply into the reserves.

The only German aircraft able to continue operating at will were the jet propelled types, but these existed in such small numbers that they could achieve little more than a nuisance value against the Allied ground troops. For example, the Ar 234's of K.G. 76 and the Me 262 bombers of K.G. 51 flew a number of single aircraft operations against American troops in the Ardennes. The U.S. air force's reaction to these was immediate and formidable: standing patrols at 5,000 feet, 10,000 and 15,000 feet, and when a jet showed up they all pounced on it. Even so the swift bombers proved to be very difficult targets, and losses were few and far between. If the German bombing caused little damage, at least these 'decoy duck' tactics tied down large numbers of American fighters which might themselves have been attacking ground targets; it was the nearest thing to air cover the weary German troops were to get during the closing months of the war.

Only the two home defence *Gruppen* fully equipped with the Me 262 fighter, the Third *Gruppe* of J.G. 7 and *Jagdverband* 44,* were in any position to contest the Allied air superiority over Germany, and these put up a spirited resistance to the very end. Adolf Galland, the recently deposed General in charge of fighters, commanded JV 44; he collected around him many of the finest German pilots, and in the hands of such men the Me 262's scored many victories during the battles with the Allied day bombers. But, like Canute, they could not stop the tide: Germany was inexorably being defeated in all three dimensions and on all fronts. On May 4th, 1945 the German land, sea and air forces in North-Western Europe surrendered, to be followed shortly afterwards by those remaining on the other fronts. The war in Europe was over.

The *Luftwaffe* had fought bravely to the finish, to its last drop of fuel if not to its last aircraft or pilot. When the end came there were still some 3,500 aircraft remaining, but most sat at their dispersals with empty tanks. Between September 1st, 1939 and February 28th, 1945, the last date for which reliable figures exist, the force had lost 44,065 aircrewmen killed, 28,200 wounded and 27,610 prisoners or missing.

Now the victorious Allies set about obliterating every last trace of the vanquished air force. For the men, the prison cages. For some of the aircraft— new ones, the interesting ones, the curiosities—a place at the various foreign testing centres; a few more went to serve in the less well-off air forces amongst the victors; but for the great majority of the aircraft, the ignominy of the scrapheap. Those installations of use to the occupying powers were kept, the remainder were blown up or otherwise dismantled.

* Literally 'Fighter Unit 44', this was an *ad hoc* unit formed to operate Me 262's in the fighter role.

So died the *Luftwaffe*, just ten years after it had come into the open. In its time it had been the terror of Europe. But when it was drawn into a long war of attrition with enemies of equal ability and greater resources, the force was beaten to its knees.

Appendix A

Operational Command of the *Luftwaffe*

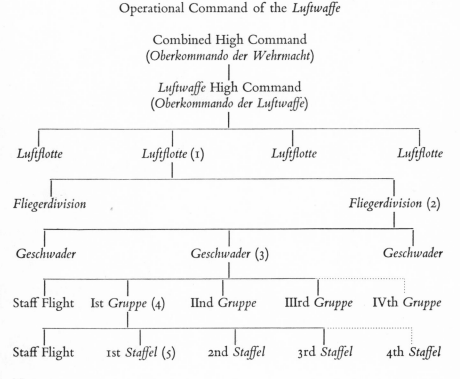

Combined High Command
(*Oberkommando der Wehrmacht*)

Luftwaffe High Command
(*Oberkommando der Luftwaffe*)

Luftflotte   *Luftflotte* (1)   *Luftflotte*   *Luftflotte*

Fliegerdivision   *Fliegerdivision* (2)

Geschwader   *Geschwader* (3)   *Geschwader*

Staff Flight   Ist *Gruppe* (4)   IInd *Gruppe*   IIIrd *Gruppe*   IVth *Gruppe*

Staff Flight   1st *Staffel* (5)   2nd *Staffel*   3rd *Staffel*   4th *Staffel*

Notes:

(1) *Luftflotten*, numbered 1, 2, 3, 4, and 5, later 6 also. These were allocated to cover a set geographical area, and comprised all types of flying units; its strength could be anything between 200 and 1,300 aircraft, depending upon the importance of the area.

(2) The *Fliegerdivision*, later renamed *Fliegerkorps*, could operate either within or independent of a *Luftflotte*. It too comprised all types of flying units; its strength could be anywhere between 200 and 750 aircraft, depending upon the importance of its area.

(3) The *Geschwader* was the largest German formation to have a nominal fixed strength; it usually comprised 90 aircraft in three *Gruppen* plus a Staff Flight with four. Within a *Geschwader* the aircraft were normally confined to one role, i.e. *Jagdgeschwader* (J.G.), fighters, *Nachtjagd-* (N.J.G.)—night fighters, *Zerstoerer-* (Z.G.)—heavy fighters, *Kampf-* (K.G.)—bombers, *Stuka-* (St. G.)—dive bombers, *Schlacht-* (S.G.)—ground attack.

61

(4) A *Gruppe* usually comprised 27 aircraft in three *Staffeln*, and a Staff Flight with three.　The IVth *Gruppe* was a training unit, attached to a bomber *Geschwader*.

(5) The *Staffel* comprised nine aircraft.　Usually there were three *Staffeln* in a *Gruppe*, but sometimes a fourth was added.

Appendix B

Wartime Production of the More Important German Combat Aircraft, By Type

ARADO 196 (*single-engined reconnaissance floatplane*), 435.

ARADO 234 (*twin-jet bomber and reconnaissance*), 214.

BLOHM UND VOSS 138 (*three-engined reconnaissance flying boat*), 276.

DORNIER 17 (*twin-engined bomber, reconnaissance and intruder*), 506.

DORNIER 215 (*twin-engined reconnaissance*), 101.

DORNIER 217 (*twin-engined bomber, reconnaissance, and night fighter*), 1,730.

DORNIER 24 (*three-engined reconnaissance flying boat*), 135.

FIESLER 156 (*single-engined communications*), 2,549.

FOCKE-WULF 190 (*single-engined fighter and ground attack*), 20,001.

FOCKE-WULF 200 (*four-engined long-range reconnaissance bomber*), 263.

FOCKE-WULF 189 (*twin-engined reconnaissance*), 846.

HEINKEL 111 (*twin-engined bomber, later used as a transport*), 5,656.

HEINKEL 115 (*twin-engined seaplane torpedo bomber and reconnaissance*), 269.

HEINKEL 177 (*four-engined long-range bomber*), 1,146.

HEINKEL 219 (*twin-engined night fighter*), 268.

HENSCHEL 126 (*single-engined reconnaissance*), 510.

HENSCHEL 129 (*twin-engined ground attack*), 841.

JUNKERS 52 (*three-engined transport, also used for advanced training*), 2,804.

JUNKERS 87 (*single-engined dive bomber*), 4,881.

JUNKERS 88 (*twin-engined bomber, ground attack, night fighter and reconnaissance*), 15,000.

JUNKERS 188 (*twin-engined bomber*), 1,036.

MESSERSCHMITT 109 (*single-engined fighter, reconnaissance*), 30,480.

MESSERSCHMITT 110 (*twin-engined fighter, night fighter, reconnaissance*), 5,762.

MESSERSCHMITT 210 (*twin-engined fighter, fighter bomber, reconnaissance*), 348.

MESSERSCHMITT 262 (*twin-engined jet fighter, fighter bomber, and night fighter*), 1,294.

MESSERSCHMITT 323 (*six-engined transport*), 201.

MESSERSCHMITT 410 (*twin-engined bomber, reconnaissance, and heavy fighter*), 1,013.

Appendix C

Equivalent Commissioned Ranks

Luftwaffe	*Royal Air Force*	*United States Air Force*
Leutnant	Pilot Officer	Second Lieutenant
Oberleutnant	Flying Officer	Lieutenant
Hauptmann	Flight Lieutenant	Captain
Major	Squadron Leader	Major
Oberstleutnant	Wing Commander	Lieutenant Colonel
Oberst	Group Captain	Colonel
Generalmajor	Air Commodore	Brigadier General
Generalleutnant	Air Vice Marshal	Major General
General	Air Marshal	Lieutenant General
Generaloberst	Air Chief Marshal	General
Generalfeldmarschall	Marshal of the Royal Air Force	General of the Air Force

The Commander in Chief of the new *Luftwaffe*, Hermann Goering, pictured as he liked to think of himself: a fighter ace of World War I with twenty victories to his credit. A brave and resourceful pilot, Goering ended the war as commander of the elite Richthofen *Geschwader*

The architect of the new air force was Erhard Milch, Goering's deputy

The fledgling *Luftwaffe* drew heavily upon the German airline *Lufthansa* for both men and training facilities. A Junkers G33 airliner of *Lufthansa* pictured at Croydon in 1932

A formation of Heinkel 60 floatplanes, pictured before the *Luftwaffe* came into the open. Note that these machines all bear civil markings

[*Radio Times Hulton Picture Library*

At first the emphasis in the new *Luft-waffe* was on training, and under the initial plan half the numerical strength of the force was in training machines. Above, the Focke-Wulf 44 *Stieglitz* initial trainer; below, the Focke-Wulf 58 *Weihe* crew trainer

The initial combat types. Above, the Heinkel 51 fighter; these belonged to *Jagdgeschwader* 132. Below, Junkers 52 bombers of *Kampfgeschwader* 152; note the underneath 'dustbin' gun position

Dornier 23 bombers. Those in the picture above belong to
Kampfgeschwader 253

Reconnaissance types: above, the Heinkel 46, a parasol wing monoplane, was the initial equipment for the short range reconnaissance units. The Heinkel 70F (below) was built in small numbers as a high speed reconnaissance aircraft

[Joos [Schliephake

The Dornier 19. This German attempt to produce a four-engined heavy bomber resulted in a machine with only a mediocre performance. Three were built in 1936, but the type was rejected in favour of greater numbers of twin engined bombers

These two photographs show the panache and spectacle of the pre-war German parades. Above, Goering raises his baton in salute as the standards are marched past. Right, Dornier 17's trail smoke as they fly low over the arena at Nuremburg

[Radio Times Hulton Picture Library

Adolf Hitler's personal aircraft, a Focke-Wulf 200. This machine was fitted with a special armoured seat for the Nazi leader   [Schliephake

Hitler arrives in Vienna, after the bloodless takeover of Austria in March 1938. To his left, Generaloberst von Bock of the army; to his right Generaloberst Milch of the air force
[Radio Times Hulton Picture Library

The Junkers 86 went into service in 1936, but this bomber was powered by diesel motors which proved unsatisfactory in service. The type had been almost entirely replaced in the bomber units before the war began

In 1936 the Germans had begun experimenting with radar, and by 1938 they had the *Freya* early warning set in service. This equipment, seen here, was in some respects superior to the British Chain Home set

[*Telefunken*

Henschel 123 dive bomber of St.G. 165. This was the first German type to enter large scale service in this role

[Joos

During 1936 the first of the new generation of German combat aircraft began to appear, and by 1938 most of them were in service. Left top, the Messerschmitt Bf 109B; left bottom, its cockpit layout

[Schliephake   [Messerschmitt A.G.

The Junkers 87 replaced the Hs 123 in many of the dive bomber units

[Joos

The Spanish Civil War provided the *Luftwaffe* with invaluable combat experience. Left, General-major Hugo Sperrle, the commander of the German Condor Legion in Spain. Below, Dornier 17E's over Spain

[*Imperial War Museum*
[*Selinger*

By using the most modern types it had, the *Luftwaffe* gained aerial superiority in Spain. Right above, a Heinkel 111 in action; right below, He 111's break formation before landing after a sortie

[*Obert* [*Selinger*

Luftwaffe coastal types. Left above, the He 115 minelayer and torpedo bomber. Left below, the Do 24 reconnaissance flying boat photographed in a heavy swell

[*Heinkel* [*Dornier*

Do 17E's pictured just before the war. The aircraft below bears the black disc markings painted on for an exercise

[*Selinger*

In Poland the *Luftwaffe* was able to go about its business with little interference from the army. The Ju 87 dive bomber, above, proved to be an outstanding success during this campaign. Below, groundcrewmen prepare Do 17's of Reconnaissance *Gruppe* 22 for take-off

[*Hans Obert*

Above, groundcrewmen load
550 lb bombs externally on an
He 111. Note the cardboard
whistles fitted to the tail fins
of the bombs, a measure which
was, initially, very effective
against enemy morale. Below,
an He 111 releases a stick of
110 lb bombs

After the end of the campaign in Poland both sides settled down to the 'phoney war'. One of the few notable actions fought during this time was on December 18th, 1939 when Bf 109's, above, and Bf 110's fought a pitched battle with R.A.F. Wellingtons near Wilhelmshaven. During the action twelve of the twenty-two Wellingtons were shot down; below, German soldiers guard the wreckage of one of them. Following this disaster, the R.A.F. confined almost the whole of its strategic bombing to night attacks

[*Joos*

The campaigns in Norway and Denmark saw the first airborne
assault operations ever. Here *Luftwaffe* paratroopers
prepare to board Ju 52's. Over Norway the long range
Bf 110's (below) proved very useful in establishing air
superiority, especially during the early part of the campaign

[*Joos*

Above, He 111's of the Third *Gruppe* of K.G. 26 operating
from a frozen lake near Trondheim during the Norwegian
campaign. Below, two British ships caught and bombed by
III/K.G. 26 during the evacuation from Narvik

One of the striking innovations during the campaign in the
west was the use of glider borne assault troops, in particular
during the capture of the Belgian Fort Eben Emael. Above,
a D.F.S. 230 glider of the type that carried the men to their
objective. Below, *Luftwaffe* assault pioneers pictured after
the capture of the Fort

At first light on May 10th, 1940 the *Luftwaffe* launched powerful attacks on British and French, Belgian and Dutch airfields, and destroyed many aircraft on the ground. Above, attempts to ward off the German attacks by the few and badly organised forces remaining met with little success; a German soldier inspects a shot down Hurricane. Below, Do 17's of K.G. 2 in battle formation

[*Selinger*

The Battle of Britain marked the first real setback for the *Luftwaffe*. Above, groundcrewmen loading bombs, nose upwards, into an He 111; below, preparing Ju 88's for action

Ju 88's, above, climb to altitude over France. Below, Do 17's
assembled in attack formation

He 111's in battle formation. Before and during the early part of the war there was a widely held belief that the cross-fire from such a formation would be strong enough to ward off determined fighter attacks. Each air force in turn learned that this was not so

Above, one of the German disappointments during the Battle
was the failure of the Bf 110 as an escort fighter, because it
lacked the agility of the British single engined fighters

[Joos

Left, senior German commanders pictured during the Battle
of Britain. Left to right: Generaloberst Hans Jeschonek,
the Chief of Air Staff; Generalfeldmarschall Albert Kesselring, commander of *Luftflotte 2*; General Speidel, Kesselring's
chief of staff; General Bruno Loerzer, commander of *Fliegerkorps* II which was part of *Luftflotte 2*

Occasionally German day bombers succeeded in penetrating
the defences and reached the London area. Left, an He 111
over central London on September 7th.   Above, oil storage
tanks at Newhaven, on the Thames, burn after being bombed
[Imperial War Museum

Left, the German daylight attacks on Britain were met by the full force of R.A.F. Fighter Command.
Above, He 111's under fire. Below, a fighter closes in on the tail of a Do 17

Imperial War Museum

Above, a Do 17 falls, its starboard motor on fire. Below, an He 111 of K.G. 26 under guard after being shot down over Britain

Often bombers returned to France with serious damage, or with dead or dying crewmen. This He 111 belonged to K.G. 54

[Obert

Following the defeat of their day bombers over Britain, the Germans launched a number of attacks using Bf 109's in the fighter bomber role, each with a single 550 lb bomb. The attacks achieved little

[Schliephake

The daylight bombing offensive petered out in October 1940,
by which time the night attacks were in full swing. Above,
aircrewmen board an He 111 of K.G. 4 loaded with two
2,200 lb bombs. Below, a Ju 88 with an external load of
four 550 lb bombs taxies out to take off

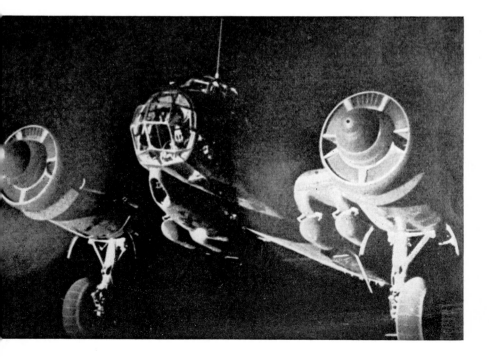

Above, Oberst Edgar Petersen commanded the anti-shipping unit K.G. 40, which caused serious losses to shipping in the ill-protected convoys during 1940 and the beginning of 1941

Left top, an He 111 takes off into the night, bound for Britain

Left bottom, on the night of November 14th, 1940 the German pathfinder unit *Kampfgruppe* 100, equipped with the precision bombing *X-Geraet*, led the bomber force during the devastating attack on Coventry. In this picture of a crashed He 111 of K.Gr. 100, the extra two aerials for the *X-Geraet* may be seen on the rear fuselage.

Aircrewmen of K.G. 40 prepare to board their Condor for
an oversea flight

An Fw 200 Condor of K.G. 40. Although the Condors took a serious toll of shipping in their heyday, it was rare for more than eight of these frail machines to be serviceable at any one time

Two very near misses on a troopship after an attack by a Condor. At the instant this picture was taken the aircraft was little higher than the ship's masts

Picture with a story. On the evening of January 17th, 1941 eleven He 111's of K.G. 26 set out from Benghazi and made an unsuccessful attack on shipping in the Suez Canal. During the return flight the Heinkels ran into strong head winds. One by one the bombers, their tanks dry, crash landed in the desert; only one made it back to Benghazi. In this remarkable photograph the force commander Major Martin Harlinghausen, right, and the machine's pilot, Hauptmann Robert Kowalewski, left, stand by their wrecked machine shortly before they set fire to it and began their walk back to the coast. The men had no water, a little bread and—worse than useless from the point of view of survival—a bottle of cognac. Unknown to the four, safety lay 175 miles away; after a five day trek the men, dehydrated and near to death, were extremely lucky to be seen and picked up by a searching Ju 52

The campaign in the Balkans in the spring of 1941 showed that the *Luftwaffe* could still hit hard after the Battle of Britain. Above, German groundcrewmen hand crank to motor of a Bf 109 prior to ground running. Below, the long range Bf 110's again proved their worth during this campaign; these belonged to Z.G. 26 [Joos

Generaloberst Student, left, commanded the *Luftwaffe* paratroops division, and was the man who put forward the idea of an airborne invasion of Crete. But during this action losses in both men and aircraft were heavy, and never again did the Germans launch a large scale airborne operation; below, a Ju 52 goes down in flames after being struck by anti-aircraft fire

[*Imperial War Museum*

The fighter squadron that never was. German propaganda photographs intended to show the Heinkel 100 fighter in large scale service, although only a handful was ever built. The twelve pre-production machines were painted in various spurious unit markings, and photographed in lines. Right, a line-up of these aircraft, captioned as 'Heinkel 113's'; right below, one of the Heinkels, repainted with the badge of a non-existent night fighter unit. The ruse was successful, and there are many reports of Allied pilots having done battle with 'Heinkel 113's'

Left, the famous German woman pilot Hanna Reitsch, who carried out flight testing on many new aircraft for the *Luftwaffe*. Below, she shakes Hitler's hand after he had presented her with the Iron Cross for her work

[*Radio Times Hulton Picture Library*]

Some of the most ferocious air-sea battles of the war were fought when the British attempted to push convoys through the German blockade of Malta. Above, a Ju 88 of III/K.G. 30, one of the units which fought during these actions. Below, this German photograph shows an aircraft carrier and a cruiser weaving desperately to avoid the bombs. Note the density of the A.A. fire, and the smoke screen from the carrier

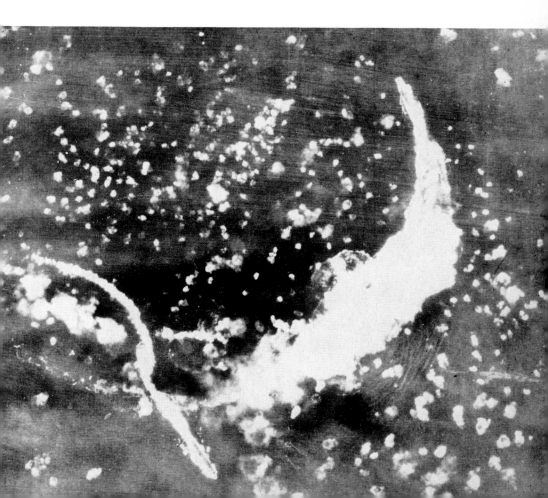

One of the features of the Russian campaign was the lavish
use made of aerial reconnaissance in the early stages. Above,
the Henschel 126; below, the later Focke-Wulf 189. Both
of these were short range reconnaissance types

[Imperial War Museum

During the summer of 1941 the Germans advanced rapidly into Russia. Above, a Fieseler 156 takes off from a road in Russia; this type was widely used for army co-operation and communications work. In the early stages the Germans were able to inflict serious losses on the Red Air Force, both in the air and on the ground. Below, groundcrewmen paint another victory bar on the tail of a Bf 109

Loading aircraft with 550 lb bombs prior to attacks on targets in Russia. Above, to a Ju 87, left, to an He 111

Above right, the Ju 88 dive bomber and reconnaissance aircraft was employed in large numbers on the Russian front. Below right, mobile lifting tackle is used to remove the engine of a Ju 88, in the open

Generals 'Mud' and 'Winter' struck before the German troops could gain decisive victory in Russia. Above, ground-crewmen use inflated air bags in an attempt to get a stranded Ju 88 out of the mud. Below, a Bf 109 with full tanks, abandoned in the snow during the Russian counter-offensive

[*Imperial War Museum*

The Russian Army's habit of firing at enemy aircraft with all available weapons resulted in the expenditure of vast quantities of ammunition, but in the long run it also caused the Germans serious losses. Here Russian soldiers examine a shot down Bf 109

With the exception of the Italians, Germany's allies became more and more dependent upon her for aircraft as the war progressed. This Bf 109 was operated by the Rumanian air force.

During 1941 two important new types entered service with the *Luftwaffe*, the Focke-Wulf 190, above, and the Dornier 217, below. The former was a completely new design, while the latter was a greatly improved Do 17

[*Imperial War Museum*

Two types on which great hopes had been placed, but which suffered serious teething troubles. Above, the Me 210, intended as a replacement for the Bf 110 as a long range fighter and fighter bomber, and the Ju 87 as a dive bomber and close support aircraft as well; in the event only its much modified successor, the Me 410, entered service in small numbers in 1943. Below, the He 177 heavy bomber, intended to replace the Fw 200, the He 111 and many of the Ju 88 bombers. Despite its appearance this was a four engined aircraft, with two in-line engines coupled together in each engine nacelle. The arrangement gave constant trouble, and the He 177 did not go into action in useful numbers until the end of 1943

[Imperial War Museum

During the war the Germans took a great interest in captured foreign aircraft. Here a Whitley bomber which had crashed in the sea is raised, and brought ashore

This Stirling was captured after a forced landing in occupied Europe, in which its nose was damaged. A piece of canvas was lashed over the nose section and the machine, with crosses painted on, was flight tested by the German proving unit at Rechlin

Above, German groundcrewmen load an He 111 with practice torpedoes at the training airfield at Grossenbrode. These aircraft inflicted heavy losses on convoys taking munitions to Russia round the north of Norway. Below, He 111's of K.G. 26, and Ju 88's of K.G. 30, in action against convoy PQ 18

[Selinger [Imperial War Museum

During 1942 the war in North Africa reached its climax. Two German units which were engaged in this theatre were J.G. 27, with Bf 109E's, above, later Bf 109F's, and St.G. 3 with Ju 87's, below

[Joos [Imperial War Museum

During the disastrous attempt to supply the German troops at Stalingrad from the air, units equipped with the Ju 52 transport, above, bore the greater part of the burden and suffered the greatest losses. Below, supply canisters parachute down.

[Schliephake   [Baetcher

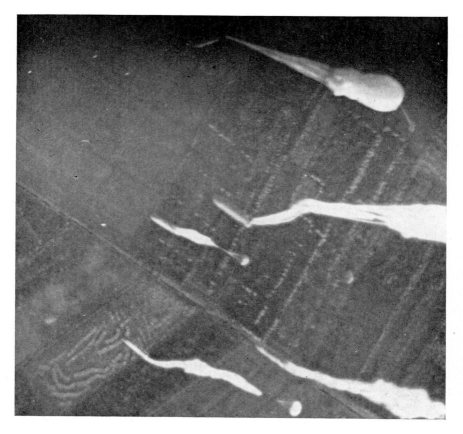

Two advanced bombers, designed to fulfil the *Luftwaffe* requirement for a high speed, high flying medium range aircraft to replace the Ju 88 and the He 111; the Junkers 288, above, and the Focke-Wulf 191, below. By the beginning of 1943 both types were well into the flight test stage. But both suffered from serious teething troubles and this, coupled with the growing shortages of aluminium and other non-ferrous metals, resulted in their cancellation

[*Schliephake*

Generalfeldmarschall Milch, second from the right, was responsible for the impressive rise in aircraft production between 1942 and 1944. He is pictured here with Goering, centre. On the far right is Oberst Petersen, the director of Air Force Research

[Petersen

Fw 190's on the production line at
Marienburg

During the initial stages of the battle of Tunisia the
Luftwaffe was able to gain, temporarily, a measure
of air superiority over the Allied air forces.
Above, a Ju 87 dive bomber, escorted by five
Italian Macchi fighters.   Below, an Hs 129 comes in
low to attack British forward positions

[Imperial War Museum

Two types used a great deal in support of German
naval units operating in the Mediterranean.
Above, the Arado 196, a coastal reconnaissance
aircraft often employed on anti-submarine duties
around Axis convoys. Below, a Ju 52 fitted with a
special loop for exploding magnetic mines from
the air

During the rapid movement of reinforcements into Tunisia, the Germans made full use of their air transport organisation. As usual, it was the Ju 52's, above, which bore the brunt of the work, but a few of the giant six-engined Me 323's were also used (below)

[*Schliephake*

Towards the end of the North African campaign the Germans
became more and more dependent upon supplies airlifted in,
but transport units operating in the face of the growing Allied
air superiority suffered heavy losses. Above, a Bf 110 escorts
Ju 52's. Below, an Me 323 under attack, shortly before it was
shot down by an Allied fighter

[Joos [Imperial War Museum

Except its initial and final stages, the campaign in the east saw He 111 units being used in an almost continual series of close-support operations for the German army, in which they suffered serious losses. Above, He 111's of I/K.G. 100 parked near the bomb dump at an airfield in Russia. Below, a 5,500 lb bomb about to be loaded on to an He 111

[Baetcher

He 111's over Russia.   The machine above belongs to K.G. 53

Schliephake

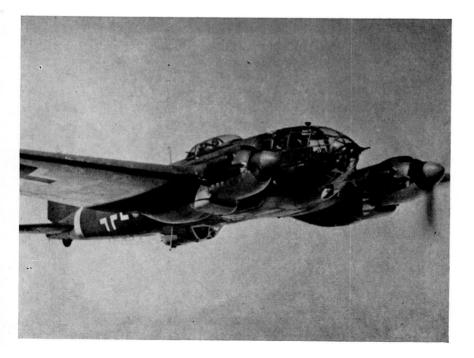

The fierce ground battles on the Eastern Front resulted in demands for specialised attack aircraft for the *Luftwaffe*. The Henschel 129, above left, was one such type. Some of these machines were fitted with the high velocity MK 103 cannon, similar to the one being examined by the author, left; this weapon fired tungsten-cored shells each weighing over a pound at 2,350 feet per second, which were able to pierce the relatively thin side and rear armour of the Russian tanks

[*Schliephake*

Above, a Ju 87 fitted with two 37 mm. *Flak* 18 cannon under the wings. Below, the Ju 88A-13, an armoured version of the much-used bomber; this machine uses a pair of 'Wateringcan' weapon canisters under the fuselage, each of which houses four machine guns fixed to fire forwards and downwards and a further four fixed to fire rearwards and downwards

[*Selinger*

During the Allied invasion of Sicily, the supporting air attacks were so heavy that the Germans had great difficulty in preventing their aircraft being destroyed on the ground. To prevent further losses, the Fw 190 fighter bombers based on Sicily were moved back to the Naples area

During the summer of 1943 the Germans often sent Ju 88
fighters into the Bay of Biscay to engage Allied patrol aircraft
hunting U-boats there. In reply, Coastal Command of the
R.A.F. sent patrols of Beaufighters and later Mosquitoes into
the area. Here a Ju 88 goes down in flames, after being
attacked by British fighters

By June 1943 the German night fighter force had a strength of 554 aircraft. For the most part these were Bf 110's and Ju 88's, but a few Do 217's, above, were also used

[*Imperial War Museum*

One of the measures taken to deepen the *Himmelbett* system of radar stations was the fighter-control ship *Togo*, intended to cover the seaward approaches to the German targets. But the British *Window* countermeasure neutralised the *Himmelbett* system, and the *Togo* spent her career in the Baltic directing fighters against Russian night raiders which did not use *Window*.

[*Imperial War Museum*

Following the success of the British *Window* tactics, the Germans were forced to introduce new measures of their own. Under the *Wild Boar* system single-engined fighters, like the Bf 109 shown above, were sent up to engage bombers illuminated by the searchlights at the target. Below, Goering inspects *Wild Boar* crews; to his left stands Major Herrmann, the originator of the system

[*Joos*   [*Herrman*

For the twin engined night fighters Colonel von Loss-berg devised the *Tame Boar* method of loosely controlled pursuit fighting.

[von Lossberg

Ground running the engines of a Bf 110 prior to a *Tame Boar* sortie

[Seeley

By the beginning of 1944 the Germans were able, by the introduction of new equipment as well as the new tactics, to overcome *Window*. The cumbersome aerial system mounted on the nose of this Bf 110 belongs to two separate radar sets. The SN-2, which used the outer aerials, was used for long range working. The Lichtenstein C-1, which used the central aerial array, was used when the target had been tracked down to short range. The German night fighters carried heavy batteries of cannon. Many pilots preferred to attack the British bombers from underneath, using upwards firing cannon as fitted to this Ju 88, below

[*Imperial War Museum*

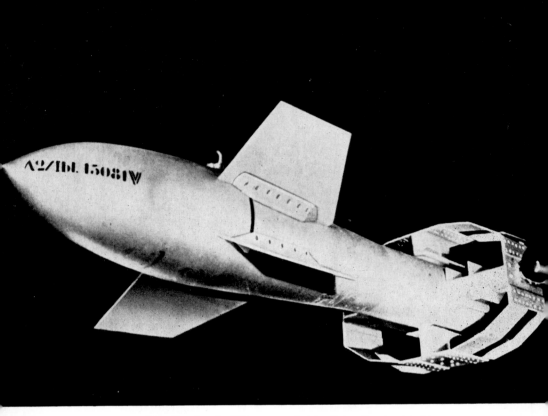

Kampfgeschwader 100, commanded by Major Bernhard Jope, below, used Fritz X guided bombs, above, with great effect against the Italian battlefleet as it made for Malta to surrender, and sank the battleship *Roma*

[Jope   [United States Air Force

The guided bombs were released from Do 217K-2's, above,
a version of the Do 217 bomber specially modified with a
longer wingspan, to enable it to climb above 20,000 feet with
a pair of these weapons. Following their success against the
Italians, Jope's men went into action against shipping off
Salerno. They hit H.M.S. *Warspite* amidships with one bomb,
and gashed her side compartments with two more. Below,
Warspite enters Malta harbour after the attack, low in the
water after taking on some 5,000 tons of it through her
fractured hull. The battleship did not see action again for
almost a year

[*Imperial War Museum*

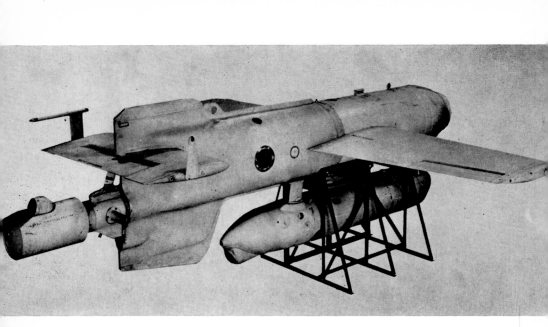

The Henschel 293 glider bomb, above, might have been very effective had it been introduced into service early in the war. But it was used only sporadically from the summer of 1943, when the scale of Allied fighter cover was usually such that attacks could not be pressed home. Below, the Hs 293 was guided on to its target by means of a simple joy-stick controller

[United States Air Force   [Trenkle

The glider bombs were carried into action by He 177's
(above, seen with one under the fuselage), or Do 217's (below)

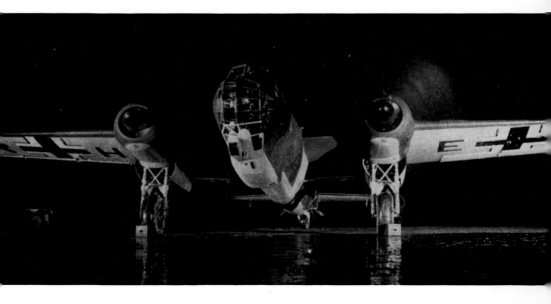

During the war the Germans conducted trials with rocket assisted take-off equipment, using several types of aircraft. Here an He 111 gets airborne with its aid

[*Schliephake*

An interesting type was the He 111Z, a 'Siamese Twin'.
Two standard He 111H's, each with an outer wing panel re-
moved, were joined together by a small stub wing mounting
a fifth engine. Twelve of these machines were assembled,
and were used in service to tow heavy transport gliders
delivering priority cargoes to the front

[Schliephake

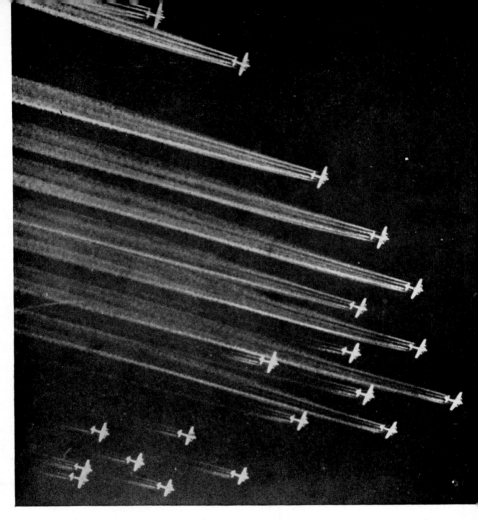

The initial phase of the American daylight bomber offensive, when they attempted to penetrate to their targets without a fighter escort, resulted in heavy losses. Above, a formation of Fortresses makes for its target at high altitude. Below, signals personnel of the *Luftwaffe* track the formation as it nears German territory

German fighters carried 210 mm. rocket mortars under their wings when they went into action against the American bombers; above, a Fw 190. Once the bombers had been damaged, and forced to leave the protective fire of the rest of the formation, they were finished off almost at leisure; below, an Fw 190 delivers a *coup de grâce* to a Fortress already on fire

The American attack on Schweinfurt on October 14th, 1943 marked the climax, and the virtual end, of the unescorted daylight bombing attacks on Germany; sixty bombers were shot down out of the 291 committed. Above and below, men of the *Luftwaffe* examine a shot down Fortress

[*Trenkle*

In addition to the sixty bombers lost during the attack on Schweinfurt, a further 138 returned to their bases in Britain with varying degrees of damage, right

[*United States Air Force*

In January 1944 the Germans launched their own bombing offensive on Britain, code-named Operation Ibex. The bulk of the attacking force comprised units flying the Do 217 (above), the He 177 (below) and the Me 410 (right above)

Also used was the Ju 88, below. However, the British night defences had improved markedly since 1941, and the *Luftwaffe* suffered heavily. This Ju 88 A-4 crashed on the Fighter Command airfield at Bradwell Bay, Essex, on April 18th, 1944 after attacking London

During the early part of 1944 the Americans again resumed their daylight attacks on Germany. Above left, an Me 410 of Z.G. 26 peels away after pressing home an attack on a Fortress; note the barrel of the 50 mm. BK 5 cannon fitted in the nose. Below left, a Fortress, its wing sheared off by hits from heavy calibre cannon shells, tumbles out of the sky. But now the American bombers enjoyed strengthening fighter cover to their targets and back, and soon it was the German fighters that were suffering heavily during the engagements. Above, an Me 410 under attack from an American escort; note the pair of launching tubes under each wing, for the 210 mm. rockets. Below, a Bf 109G pictured shortly before its destruction by a Mustang

[*United States Air Force*

During the months immediately prior to the invasion of Normandy, Allied aircraft made intensive attacks on German airfields in France. Above, Mosquitoes attacking the airfield at Gael. Below and right, wrecked German aircraft seen after the attack on Bordeaux/Merignac

[*Imperial War Museum* [*Trenkle*

When the Allied troops landed on the north coast of France, the *Luftwaffe* threw almost its entire bomber strength in the west against the bridgehead. Above, a Ju 88S of I/K.G. 66 running its engines prior to take-off from Montdidier. But the scale of air cover above the lodgement area was such that the Germans suffered heavy losses. Below, a Do 217 on fire after a fighter attack, following an attempt to deliver a glider bomb attack against Allied shipping; a few minutes later the aircraft crashed

[Altrogge   [Imperial War Museum

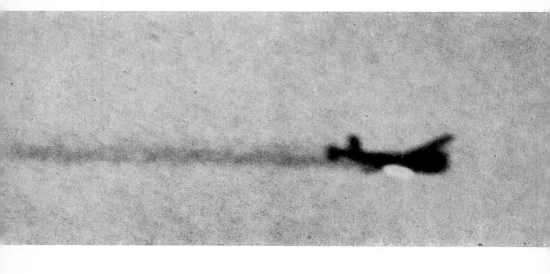

One interesting weapon for use against Allied shipping was the *Mistletoe* device, a Ju 88 laden with explosives guided to the target by a manned Bf 109 fighter mounted on top of it. Once the combination had been aligned on the target the fighter pilot released the lower component, which continued on to impact under control of its automatic pilot. Over Normandy the Allied fighters prevented the *Mistletoe* pilots pressing home their attacks. Later the Germans planned to attack battleships and aircraft carriers of the British Home Fleet at Scapa Flow, and then the Russian power stations around Moscow and Gorki, with these weapons; but in each case the attack was delayed until it was too late, and then cancelled

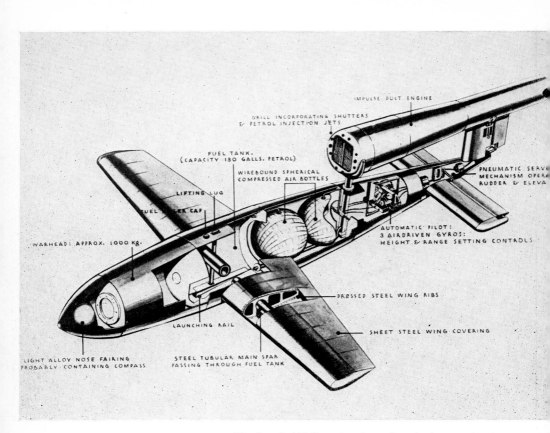

IMPULSE DUCT ENGINE

GRILL INCORPORATING SHUTTERS
& PETROL INJECTION JETS

FUEL TANK.
(CAPACITY 130 GALLS. PETROL)

WIREBOUND SPHERICAL
COMPRESSED AIR BOTTLES

PNEUMATIC SERVO
MECHANISM OPERA
RUDDER & ELEVA

LIFTING LUG

FUEL TANK CAP

AUTOMATIC PILOT:
3 AIRDRIVEN GYROS:
HEIGHT & RANGE SETTING CONTROLS

WARHEAD: APPROX. 1000 kg.

PRESSED STEEL WING RIBS

SHEET STEEL WING COVERING

LAUNCHING RAIL

LIGHT ALLOY NOSE FAIRING
PROBABLY CONTAINING COMPASS

STEEL TUBULAR MAIN SPAR
PASSING THROUGH FUEL TANK

The first Fi 103 flying bomb was launched against London on
the evening of June 12th, 1944, and by the beginning of
September more than 8,500 of these weapons had been fired
at the British capital. Above, the Fiesler 103, more generally
known in Britain as the V1. Below, men of the *Luftwaffe*
moving partially assembled Fi 103's up to the launching sites,
for preparation for firing

[*Imperial War Museum*

By the beginning cf 1944 the Ju 87 dive bomber had been
replaced in most units by ground attack versions of the
Fw 190. This machine is seen here fitted with three 550 lb
bombs   [Schliephake

The Bf 109G-12, two seater training version of the much used
fighter. The shortage of such high performance types at the
German training units was one of the reasons for the short-
comings in *Luftwaffe* fighter pilots during the closing stages
of the war   [Schliephake

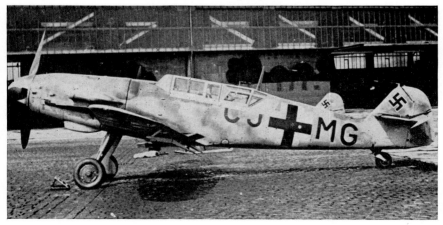

Once the German fighter opposition had been rendered ineffective, the British and American heavy bombers concentrated on the Achilles' heel of the German war economy: oil. Above, smashed oil tanks near Hanover; below, the wrecked synthetic oil plant at Boehlen, following a heavy attack by the R.A.F.

[Imperial War Museum

Gradually the fuel famine began to strangle the *Luftwaffe* as a fighting force. First the training, bomber and reconnaissance units suffered, later the fighter bombers and day and night fighters as well. Above, a Bf 110 night fighter grounded for want of fuel. When the night fighters did get off the ground, they became the prey of long-range Mosquito intruders which accompanied the British bomber attacks; below, a Bf 110 falling in flames after being engaged by a British night fighter

[*Seeley*

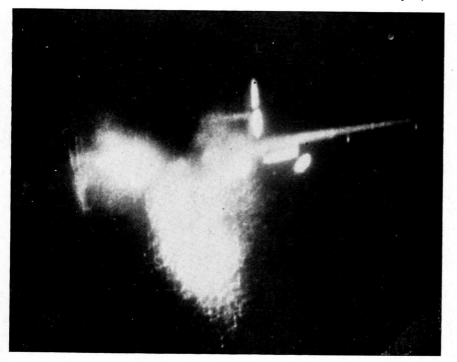

With the German fighter
opposition almost neutralised
by the American escort
fighters, the main German
defence was provided by anti-
aircraft guns at the targets.
Right, a 128 mm. gun,
manned by *Luftwaffe* personnel. Generally the guns
were able to do no more than
force the bombers to fly high,
where accurate bomb aiming
was difficult, and cause shrap-
nel damage. But a direct hit
or a very near miss would
cause a bomber to disintegrate;
below, a puff of smoke is all
that remains of a Fortress hit
by heavy flak near Berlin
[United States Air Force
[Imperial War Museum

Some ace pilots of the *Luftwaffe*. Major Gerhard Barkhorn, left, flew fighters and ended the war credited with 301 victories; today he serves with the present *Luftwaffe*. Major Heinz-Wolfgang Schnaufer, below, the top scoring night fighter pilot with 121 kills; he was killed in a road accident in France in 1950. Hauptmann, later Major, Hans-Georg Baetcher, below right, flew 658 *operational* sorties on twin engined bombers—probably a greater number than any other pilot in the world; today he is manager of an office equipment company in Berlin. These totals might seem to British or American readers incredible, but it should be remembered that in the *Luftwaffe* there was no such thing as a 'rest' job between operational tours. Aircrewmen flew on operations until they were killed, wounded, or promoted out of the job; the only planned breaks from operational flying were during the men's leave periods. Evened out over a period of up to six years the totals are high, but not incredibly so

[*Imperial War Museum* [*Baetcher*

The Me 262 jet fighter could have achieved great things had it been used in large numbers against the American bomber formations, but instead Hitler insisted that it be used initially as a fighter bomber. On this machine, which belonged to K.G. 51, the bomb racks may be seen under the nose; the type became operational as a fighter bomber only in October 1944

[*Schliephake*

On New Year's Day 1945 the Germans launched their all-out attack on the Allied forward airfields. But such was the strength of the ground defences, that the Germans suffered heavy losses during the attack. Below, a crashed Fw 190

[*Obert*

During the Ardennes battles at the end of 1944 and the beginning of 1945, the Arado 234 jet bombers of K.G. 76 operated in small numbers. Above, *Luftwaffe* groundcrewmen refuel an Arado; the low grade petrol used by the jets was the only type of aviation fuel not in very short supply at this stage. Centre, Major Robert Kowalewski, the commander of the world's first true jet bomber unit; today he manages an iron foundry in the Ruhr. Below, an Arado ready for take-off; the periscope fitted to the cockpit was used for rear vision, and also as a sight during the shallow dive attacks

[*Kowalewski*

During the closing stages of the war the few Me 262 units put up a spirited resistance against the Allied bomber formations, but there was little else. Above, Me 262's await the order to take off. Centre, Generalmajor Adolf Galland, the commander of the elite fighter unit J.V. 44 which flew Me 262's. Below, an Me 262 shows off its distinctive swept-wing form

[Baetcher [Imperial War Museum
[United States Air Force

One of the most remarkable air combat photographs even taken: an Me 262 pictured seconds before it was shot down by the photographing Mustang. In front of the jet is a second Mustang, under attack from the Messerschmitt. The cloud banks provide an idea of the horizon, and the crazy weaving of the fighters. The line across the nose of the Me 262 marks the angle of the wings of the photographic aircraft

United States Air Force

Ground-straffing Allied fighters were a constant menace to the *Luftwaffe* as the war neared its end. Above, Mustangs shoot up an airfield used by the Germans. Below, one of the fastest German piston engined fighters, the Dornier 335, seen with machine gun damage; there were great hopes for this machine, but when the end came only eleven had been built

In an effort to discourage the low flying attackers, the Germans established powerful flak lanes along the approach lines to their airfields. Above, a 37 mm. light anti-aircraft gun; the man standing at the rear is holding a small optical range-finder. When the Allies found them, the airfields used by the jets came in for special attention. The task of the German piston engined fighter units, when there was fuel, was often to protect the jets during take-off and landing. One of the types introduced towards the end and used for this purpose was the Fw 190D, an improved version of the Fw 190 with a performance closely comparable with the British Tempest and the American Mustang

[Imperial War Museum   [Schliephake

Two last-ditch attempts by the Germans to wrest air superiority from the Allies. Above left, the Me 163 rocket fighter, a machine with an impressive speed and altitude performance, but also a disconcerting habit of exploding on landing if there was any fuel remaining in its tanks. Due to a shortage of the special fuel necessary for the rocket motor, this type saw action only rarely. Below left, sparsely appointed cockpit of the Me 163; compare the simplicity of the instrumentation of the rocket fighter with that of the Bf 109 on page 76. Above and below, the He 162, an attempt to provide a simple and cheap jet fighter in large numbers and quickly. The type was rushed into service with J.G. 1 in the last weeks of the war, before it had been properly tested; its handling characteristics were in some respects vicious, and the fighter was more dangerous to friend than foe

[*Schliephake*

To the very end of the war the Germans worked hard to introduce revolutionary new weapons. The D.F.S. 228 rocket-powered reconnaissance aircraft was to have been carried to the edge of enemy defences on the back of a Do 217, then released. The pilot of the reconnaissance machine then fired his rocket and climbed to 40,000 feet, after which he fired it in short bursts so that he reached his target at about this altitude. His mission completed, the pilot was to use up the rest of his fuel, then glide back to friendly territory. When the war ended, powered flight trials of the D.F.S. 228 were about to begin

Above and below, as the Allied forces advanced deeper and deeper into Germany they found hundreds of aircraft wrecked either by the retreating Germans or the advancing Allies

[United States Air Force   [Imperial War Museum

Others could easily have been made flyable, but they sat on the ground with empty tanks. Within a few months of the end of the war almost the entire aircraft strength of the *Luftwaffe* had been consigned to the scrapheap

[*Imperial War Museum*

Before the war Goering had said that he would see to it that no bombs fell on the Ruhr. Few prophets were ever to be proved more wrong. Above, the Krupp works at Essen, pictured in 1945. During the course of the war the works had been attacked and repaired many times, but following a particularly heavy air raid in October 1944 all production ceased

Imperial War Museum

Hermann Goering, pictured in the dock at the International
Military Tribunal held at Nuremburg after the war. On
October 1st, 1946 he was sentenced to death by hanging, but
he committed suicide by taking poison on October 16th, the
day before the sentence was to have been carried out

[Radio Times Hulton Picture Library